Drinking
with My Dog

Drinking with My Dog

THE CANINE LOVER'S COCKTAIL BOOK

Natalie Bovis

Illustrated by Rae Ritchie

RUNNING PRESS

PHILADELPHIA

Running Press
Hachette Book Group
1290 Avenue of the Americas, New York, NY 10104
www.runningpress.com
@Running_Press

Printed in China

First Edition: January 2023

Published by Running Press, an imprint of Perseus Books, LLC,
a subsidiary of Hachette Book Group, Inc. The Running Press name and logo
are trademarks of the Hachette Book Group.

The Hachette Speakers Bureau provides a wide range of authors for speaking events.
To find out more, go to www.hachettespeakersbureau.com or call (866) 376-6591.

The publisher is not responsible for websites (or their content) that
are not owned by the publisher.

Print book cover and interior design by Frances J. Soo Ping Chow.
Stock illustrations on pages 2 and 4 copyright © Getty Images/Anna Suslina

Library of Congress Control Number: 2022936510

ISBNs: 978-0-7624-8022-7 (hardcover), 978-0-7624-8023-4 (ebook)

RRD-S

10 9 8 7 6 5 4 3 2 1

This book is dedicated to people who love dogs
and advocate for their well-being.

. . . .

Let's raise a glass to volunteers, fosters, veterinarians, adopters,
and rescue groups saving their lives.

. . . .

Let's toast everyone who donates their time and
resources to ending animal cruelty, protecting endangered species,
and maintaining the Earth's natural spaces where dogs,
both wild and domesticated, roam.

. . . .

Finally, I thank *you* for buying *Drinking with My Dog*.
Together, we can raise awareness and take action for dogs in need.

Contents

INTRODUCTION...IX

"

I'M NOT DRINKING ALONE;
I'M DRINKING WITH MY DOG!

"

—THE LIQUID MUSE

Introduction

SINCE THE DAWN OF HUMANITY, DOGS HAVE BEEN A PART OF our lives. All the furry floofs we love and live with today descend from some form of prehistoric wolflike canid who migrated across the Earth, as did early hominids. At some point along the way, both our predecessors looked at each other and decided they could, perhaps, create mutually beneficial alliances. And, just like that (well, okay, *sort of* just like that), dogs became our most trusted and loyal friends. Some people might even argue that they are also our most toast-worthy ones.

In more recent memory, when the world ground to a halt and we locked ourselves indoors, many folks instinctively adopted a canine companion to ease the isolation. Meanwhile, as our computer screens kept us connected with our communities, social media allowed us to show off our respective versions of a "quarantini."

If there is one takeaway from forced isolation, it's that dogs *and* drinks make anything more bearable! My dog Lula was only too happy that instead of zooming off to happy hour with friends, I was having Zoom cocktail parties from home with her by my side.

We have so much to learn from and about dogs. Did you know that there are more than four hundred dog breeds in the world and—of the one billion canines that roam the planet—only one-quarter are pets? Dogs are intelligent, communicative beings, and in the coming pages, you will get to know them better. In addition to dozens of delicious cocktails, this book is dripping with fun facts about dog breeds and doggie trivia and history.

You'll read celebrity pup stories, get a peek at the dogs who've lived with world leaders, and discover fun facts about dogs who still live in the wild all around the planet. Each chapter includes drink recipes honoring our furry friends, as well as plenty of home bartending tips. There's also a whole section of dog-themed drinks to serve at year-round *paw*lidays and a guide to help you create a signature cocktail in your dog's honor, whether you are shaking up your first cocktail ever or already have mad skills in mixology. Each recipe yields one drink, unless otherwise noted, and you will also find tips on making big batches for a party.

And this book saves lives by raising awareness! As the guardians of our own dogs and guardian angels of those in need, we can share stories about the canines who live on the planet with us. Getting to know these creatures more intimately inspires more people to advocate, volunteer, and donate to help them. I raise money for animal rescues through The Liquid Muse events and I hope to clink glasses with pet lovers and cocktail enthusiasts at book signings, fundraisers, and pet-friendly pop-up parties around the world. Now, let's mix some cocktails in honor of our dogs, and stir up some good times together.

> WE DOMESTICATED THESE ANIMALS TO DEPEND ON US
> FOR EVERYTHING. IT IS OUR RESPONSIBILITY
> TO TAKE CARE OF THEM AND TREAT THEM WITH THE LOVE
> AND RESPECT THEY DESERVE. THEY ARE SENTIENT BEINGS.
> EVERY DOG STORY I WRITE IS A LOVE LETTER
> BETWEEN HUMANS AND DOGS.

—W. BRUCE CAMERON,
AUTHOR OF *A DOG'S PURPOSE*

"

IF YOU ELIMINATE SMOKING AND GAMBLING,
YOU WILL BE AMAZED TO FIND THAT ALMOST ALL
AN ENGLISHMAN'S PLEASURES CAN BE,
AND MOSTLY ARE, SHARED BY HIS DOG.

"

—GEORGE BERNARD SHAW,
PLAYWRIGHT

CHAPTER
1

YOUR HOME BAR

OBVIOUSLY, YOUR POOCH WON'T BE DRINKING THE HOOCH, but you might want to invite over your dog-loving human friends to taste your delicious concoctions. Making cocktails is fun, and you don't have to be an expert in the kitchen or have bartending experience to make great drinks. You can also create a charming home bar whether you're simply placing a few items on a cart in the corner of your living room or transforming your basement into the neighborhood watering hole. With a few bottles of spirits, a smattering of liqueurs, a cocktail shaker, and some fun glassware, you will show everyone that you are "top dog" when it comes to mixology.

Below, you'll find a list of glassware to round out your collection as you become a serious home bartender. Don't fret if you don't have the funds or space for all of these. Even if you served every drink in this book in a paper cup, it would still taste delicious. If you do get into the spirit of collecting, though, I suggest perusing virtual or in-person flea markets and resale stores for cool vintage pieces. Also, keep an eye out for shelter thrift stores. Many rescue groups take donations of gently used clothing, glassware, furniture, and other household items to sell in their own secondhand market stalls or shops. I have found some of my most beautiful glassware at these, and I also donate to them regularly because the money from sales helps pay for pet food and vet bills. Who doesn't love shopping for a good cause?

The glassware, bar tools, and ingredients in the following sections are a guide in case you're ready to go all out, but don't let these lists intimidate you. If you have a mason jar (instead of a cocktail shaker), a glass (of any kind), a tray of ice, some liquor, sugar, and lemons or limes, you can make many drinks in this book. And, at the risk of restating the obvious, do not give alcohol to your dog. All ingredients throughout this book are meant for human consumption only.

GLASSWARE

| BAR MUG | CHAMPAGNE FLUTE | COCKTAIL COUPE | HIGHBALL GLASS | COCKTAIL GLASS | RED WINE GLASS | ROCKS GLASS | WHITE WINE GLASS |

BAR MUG • A thick glass with a handle for cold or warm drinks.

CHAMPAGNE FLUTE • A long, narrow, stemmed glass used for sparkling drinks.

COCKTAIL COUPE / COCKTAIL GLASS • The original wide-bowled Champagne glass, and also used for classic stirred cocktails.

HIGHBALL/COLLINS/TALL GLASS • Ideal for fizzy drinks, with the Collins being a bit taller than the highball. Throughout this book, wherever directions suggest "strain over fresh ice in a tall glass," you can use a shorter highball glass, a taller Collins glass, or even a tall water glass. Whatever you have on hand will work.

MARTINI/COCKTAIL GLASS • This V-shaped cocktail glass holds every variation of "tini" drinks you can think of. It was traditionally called a "cocktail" glass, so throughout this book wherever directions suggest "strain into a cocktail glass," rest assured that you can use any kind of cocktail glass you wish.

RED WINE GLASS • A goblet with a wide rim allowing for more oxygen to react with the surface area of the wine, thereby allowing the flavors to "open."

ROCKS/DOUBLE ROCKS GLASS • A short, wide glass used for sipping spirits served neat/"up" or "on the rocks"—no ice and with ice, respectively. The double rocks is, obviously, a bit bigger than the plain rocks glass. Throughout this book, any drink that is served "up" in a cocktail glass could also be served "on the rocks" in a double rocks glass. Not everyone loves stemmed glassware, so any cocktail from a Cosmopolitan to a Martini can also be served over ice in one of these glasses.

WHITE WINE GLASS • A smaller, tulip-shaped wine glass.

KITCHEN TOOLS AND APPLIANCES

BLENDER • For blending frozen cocktails.

CUTTING BOARD AND PARING KNIFE • For cutting fruits and veggies.

GRATER • For grating ginger, nutmeg, and chocolate, for instance, and for zesting citrus peels.

ICE CUBE MOLDS • Look for trays with fun shapes or larger openings. Larger cubes melt more slowly. When making ice blocks for a punch bowl or pitcher, use a small plastic tub (such as a yogurt or cottage cheese container). You can also use tonic water or juice in place of plain water so that as it melts it adds more flavor to the big-batched drink rather than water it down.

JUICER • Freshly juiced fruits and vegetables make for more delicious cocktails.

MEASURING CUP • For measuring batched drinks.

PEELER • For taking the skins off fruits and veggies; helpful for making lemon or lime twists.

SMALL SAUCEPAN • For cooking syrups or purees.

BASIC BAR TOOLS

| BARSPOON | CITRUS PRESS | COCKTAIL SHAKER | ICE SCOOP | JIGGER | MUDDLER | SIEVE |

BARSPOON • Used to stir drinks, a barspoon has a long stem, with the spoon measuring about 1 teaspoon.

CITRUS PRESS • This handheld kitchen tool is shaped like half an orange, lemon, or lime, and easily squeezes out juice while holding back seeds.

COCKTAIL SHAKER • These can be both decorative and functional. A three-piece shaker has the strainer built in. A professional set of shaker tins has a larger and smaller tin that seal when shaking liquid. A Boston shaker has a tin that fits over the mouth of a pint glass. I like using these in my cocktail classes, because the students can see the ingredients as they go into the glass, making it easier to follow along. Next, we add ice and seal it with the metal tin over the top before shaking. With a Boston shaker, you will need to use a Hawthorne strainer, a round, slotted metal lid with a spring in it to hold back ice and other solids when pouring the liquid into the cocktail glass.

ICE SCOOP • When you put out a bowl of ice at a party, you will need to provide an easy and sanitary way for people to scoop it into their glass.

JIGGER • Measures liquids in ounces or milliliters.

MUDDLER • Made from wood, plastic, or metal, a muddler is essentially a pestle with a long handle to reach the bottom of a cocktail shaker and is used to press the juice or oils from fruits and herbs.

SIEVE • If you are shaking berries or muddling herbs, you might want to double strain your drink. To do this, hold a small sieve above the cocktail glass to catch little bits of mint leaves or berry seeds as the contents of the shaker pass through it, so they don't get stuck in your teeth when you take a sip.

INGREDIENTS

BAKING SPICES • Some of the recipes in this book call for spices, including cinnamon, cloves, or nutmeg.

CITRUS FRUITS • Limes, lemons, oranges, and grapefruits are just a few of the fruits you'll find in the recipes in this book.

CREAM • Typically, drinks use heavy cream, but half-and-half can be substituted for anyone watching their fat intake. For those who prefer nondairy, coconut creamer is a good substitute.

EGGS • Egg whites and egg yolks are used in a variety of drinks to add texture, mouthfeel, or froth. If you're looking for a vegan substitute for egg whites in cocktails, try aquafaba or the liquid in a can of garbanzo beans found in any supermarket. See page 15 for notes about adding raw egg to drinks.

FRESH HERBS • Mint, basil, and thyme are most common in cocktail recipes, although you'll find many recipes using other herbs, too.

FRUITS AND VEGGIES • Just about any produce can be used in drinks, making for more fresh and flavorful beverages.

SEA SALT • For rimming glasses. See page 15 for a note about rimming glasses.

SUGAR • Granulated white or raw is ideal for making syrups; note some vintage cocktail recipes call for a whole sugar cube or lump.

LAP IT UP IN STYLE

When serving cocktails, the glass is an important part of the overall drinking experience. We taste first with our eyes, so presentation counts. And, in proper cocktail-making etiquette, some drinks call for a specific type of glass. As you get into cocktail making, collecting beautiful stemware can become an obsession! I had to cut myself off from buying vintage cocktail glasses in much the same way I had to cut myself off from adopting more pets! Just as a little furry face pulls at my heartstrings, an early 1900s Champagne coupe or a mid-century gold-rimmed cocktail glass has me convincing myself that "just one more" is still not enough.

FETCH THE BOOZE!

Just as your pup's face lights up when he sees his favorite ball, you might be surprised how much you enjoy showing off your newly honed cocktail skills. And you'll find yourself seeking new "toys" at your favorite liquor store. I especially love bringing back an unusual spirit or liqueur from a trip to sip with friends while sharing travel stories—and photos of the dogs I met!—in faraway destinations. Whenever I land somewhere new, I try to understand how the people there eat and drink. It's a peek into that culture's local customs, tastes, and values. Also learning to make delicious things abroad is a very tactile way to share your experiences with your peeps back home.

Below is a list of spirits and other ingredients to create a foundation for your home bar. If this is new to you, don't get overwhelmed because you do not need to have all of these things to get started. If you're on a budget, buy bottles in increments. And, if you are particularly limited on space or funds, here is a little insider tip: Just about any cocktail can work with vodka in place of the spirit the recipe calls for. So, if you can only buy one bottle for now, make it vodka and add more spirits to your home bar as you can.

DISTILLED SPIRITS

Let's demystify alcohol so that you can walk into a liquor store or shop online with confidence. Keep in mind that "more expensive" does not always translate to "better quality." If you shop at a store that has knowledgeable clerks to help you choose the right product for you, that's even better. The following list gives you an overview of the spirits used in this book, including what they're made from and what they might taste like.

BRANDY • A distilled spirit made from fermented fruit. The most famous kind of grape brandy is Cognac, which is made in a specific region in France. Others include French Armagnac, brandy de Jerez made in Spain, and pisco, which is a South American brandy specifically made in Peru and Chile.

CACHAÇA • A form of Brazilian rum made from fermented sugarcane juice versus molasses.

GIN • In short, we can say that gin is juniper-infused vodka, because it can be made from any base, fruit or grain. As long as the base spirit is infused with juniper it qualifies as gin. Distillers may also macerate, or "stew," the liquid with citrus peels, spices, and flowers to develop more interesting flavors. There are a few distinct gin styles you can try:

London Dry Gin: Heavier in juniper flavor and tends to be a bit "drier" than other styles. It typically has citrus notes and contains no added sugars.

Modern Gin: Tends to be lighter on the juniper and may include heavier floral and fruity notes.

Sloe Gin: Essentially a liqueur rather than a gin, despite its name. It is sweetened and infused with sloe berries, which resemble a small plum or damson.

RUM • Typically made from molasses, rum can be light (un-aged) or dark (aged in wood for additional flavor and color). Spiced rum is infused with spices and vanilla. Rum can be made anywhere in the world and remains a very popular spirit in highballs, classic cocktails, and tiki drinks.

TEQUILA • Agave plants can grow in many dry climates and agave spirits are made in many places, but to call a distillate *tequila* it must be derived from the Blue Weber agave plant and produced in one of the five tequila regions in Mexico. Tequila makers mainly procure used wooden barrels from North American Bourbon distilleries, but also experiment with used barrels from French Cognac distilleries, wineries, or Spanish sherry makers to age their spirits. When any spirit sits in a barrel, it gets a deeper brownish color from the wood, and the taste of the distillate mellows as it absorbs additional flavor from both the wood and whatever was stored in it previously. With the explosion of tequila's popularity in the last decade, tequileros are getting more creative with their methods and producing more unique products. The following are the descriptors of tequila you will find on store shelves referring to how much time they spent in a barrel. In any spirit category, an older spirit is not necessarily better, but the aging will affect its flavor. Also never buy a tequila with the word "gold" on the bottle as that usually means that it has been artificially colored.

Blanco means the tequila looks clear in the bottle because it has not been aged. That said, a blanco may still have rested in a wooden barrel for up to two months.

Reposado means the tequila has rested in a wood barrel for about two to twelve months.

Añejo means "aged," and the distilled liquid has been in the barrel for at least a year.

Extra Añejo means it has been aged in the barrel for three years or more.

HAIR OF THE DOG

While some people claim that a little more liquor eases the morning after "a drink too many," what you really need is water to flush out your organs and rehydrate your body. Take small sips of water often and stay away from alcohol. When you're ready for food, I recommend the Vietnamese soup pho because the salty broth, nutritious veggies, protein, noodles, and spices are helpful for everything from a hangover to the common cold.

VODKA • Defined as an odorless, tasteless spirit, vodka can be made from any grain, vegetable, or fruit—not just potatoes as many people mistakenly believe. There are even some vodkas that are made from milk. The base material influences each vodka's mouthfeel and subtle taste. A vodka that is distilled many times is not necessarily a marker of quality, but merely indicates how many times the fermented liquid was put through the distillation process.

WHISKEY • This is a big spirits category, and there are several styles of whiskey made from different kinds of grain from all corners of the world. Note there are rules pertaining to specific whiskey styles, some of which are briefly outlined below. You'll also notice that sometimes the word *whiskey* is spelled *whisky* depending on where the spirit is made.

Bourbon Whiskey: Made in the United States from a grain mash that must be at least 51 percent corn and aged for at least two years in new charred oak barrels.

Canadian Whisky: Usually a blend that includes rye and is aged for at least two years.

Irish Whiskey: Must be made in the Emerald Isle and aged for three years in wood barrels.

Japanese Whisky: Typically made from barley, like Scotch, but experimentation is expanding in this newer and exciting category.

Rye Whiskey: Has a spicy kick and is the style of whiskey called for in many of the original whiskey cocktail recipes.

Scotch Whisky: Made from malted barley in Scotland.

FORTIFIED WINE

When wine is referred to as *fortified* it has been dosed with a little spirit and macerated with herbs and botanicals. I love sipping all varieties of fortified wines on their own, usually over a couple of ice cubes. Fortified wine is also an integral ingredient in some of our most iconic classic cocktails, such as Martinis and Manhattans. Like other kinds of wine, some fortified wines are made with specific grapes and originated in the Mediterranean region. Their rising popularity is encouraging winemakers worldwide to experiment with their own versions. Lighter fortified wines, such as dry vermouth and some sherries, are lovely *aperitifs*, or "appetite openers." Richer ones, such as port, make wonderful *digestifs* or after-dinner drinks. Keep in mind that because they are wine based, these must be refrigerated once opened or they will go rancid. Some fortified wines include:

DRY VERMOUTH • This has a white wine base and is dry (not sweet) with rich botanical flavors. It's most often used with clear spirits or on its own as an aperitif. Made at wineries around the world.

MADEIRA • These fortified wines are made on the Portuguese island of Madeira, off the coast of the Iberian Peninsula. Some varieties are dry and wonderful aperitifs and some are sweet digestifs.

MARSALA • This Italian fortified wine is made on the island of Sicily and ranges from dry to sweet.

PORT • This rich fortified wine comes from the Douro Valley in Portugal. It is most often red and sweet, although there are some drier white varietals, too.

SHERRY • This fortified wine is from Andalusia, Spain. It also has dry and sweet varietals.

SWEET VERMOUTH • With a red wine base, it's sweeter than dry vermouth, with rich botanical flavors. It is most often used with dark spirits. Could be an aperitif or digestif. Made at wineries around the world.

MORE *BARK* FOR YOUR BUCK: LAYERING FLAVORS

Once you have chosen a spirit or fortified wine as your cocktail base, the next step is to layer your drink with modifiers such as liqueurs, syrups, or bitters. These can add sweetness, floral or fruity notes, or spice. More flavor means more fun for your taste buds. Below are some ingredients to take your cocktail from merely "good dog" to "Best in Show."

LIQUEURS

A liqueur, or cordial, has a spirit base that is sweetened and flavored. Liqueurs can be fruity, floral, nutty, coffee-flavored, mint-flavored, or chocolate-flavored. They can be chilled and sipped on their own, served over ice, or mixed into a cocktail.

BITTERS

Bitters are flavor enhancers made with high-proof alcohol, bark, herbs, and other botanicals. Bitters were first created as a remedy for stomach ailments when mixed with a little water (or sparkling water). In mixology, their use can be compared to a dash of salt in food to boost flavor. A little bit goes a long way. A dash of bitters can enhance a cocktail with aroma as well, when dropped on the surface of a cocktail. Keep a bottle of each of the traditional Angostura and Peychaud's on hand if you're into classic cocktails, and experiment with the plethora of flavored bitters that have flooded liquor store shelves in recent years.

OTHER FLAVOR BOOSTERS

ROSE AND ORANGE FLOWER WATER • Often used in Middle Eastern or French cooking and baking and found in gourmet stores. These two flower essence–infused waters have subtle aromas and flavors that work beautifully in light, delicate cocktails, particularly ones with vodka or gin bases.

SPICY SAUCE • Tabasco, Sriracha, Cholula, and the like are perfect for drinks that taste better with a bit of a kick, such as the Bloody Mary or Michelada.

SYRUPS

Homemade syrups are easy to make and, of course, many ready-made ones come in a variety of flavors in stores and online. The foundation of cocktail syrups is Simple Syrup, which has a 1:1 ratio of white granulated sugar to water. To make it, simply dissolve the sugar into the water by heating them on the stove in a saucepan or in the microwave for a few minutes, stirring often, then allowing the mixture to cool. This is also the base to more creative syrups, such as the ones below. You can make any syrup sweeter and more concentrated by mixing two parts sugar to one part water. Get fancy by substituting flavored tea, fruit juice, or even wine for the water to create even more layers of flavor in a drink without incorporating a lot of ingredients.

FLORAL • To infuse floral flavors into your syrup, simply add a couple of table-spoons of dried hibiscus, lavender, rose, or jasmine flowers while cooking. Then refrigerate for several hours and strain.

HERBACEOUS • For herbal syrups, add fresh mint, thyme, or rosemary leaves while cooking, refrigerate for several hours, then strain.

ORGEAT • This almond syrup is used in some classic cocktails. Making your own is rather labor-intensive, so save yourself some trouble and choose a store-bought brand.

SPICE IS NICE • When using spices, add a few strands of saffron, grated ginger, or turmeric, for example, while cooking, refrigerate for several hours, then strain.

SWEETNESS • Store-bought agave syrup is ready to use right out of the bottle as it is quite runny. If you want honey syrup, the honey needs to be diluted with a half part of water—meaning, each ounce of honey would be diluted with ½ ounce of water. This is then heated slightly so the honey mixes with the water. Note that the mixture should be cooled before using.

GARNISHES

People love dressing up their dogs with a cute bandanna, a color-ful leash or festive collar, and sometimes even a Halloween costume. Similarly, you can also dress up your drink with a decorative garnish. The garnish enhances a drink's presen-tation, while also lending extra sparkle, aroma, and/or flavor to the drinking experience. The garnish should reflect something about the drink or event at which it is served and often signals ingredients found in the drink. In other words, a Margarita usually gets a lime wedge or wheel garnish because a whiff of fresh citrus prepares your brain for the taste about to hit your tongue.

Lemons, limes, oranges, cherries, onions, olives, candied ginger or citrus peel (cut into little strips called twists) or grated zest, edible flowers, lemongrass stalks, seasonal fruits, and vegetables are all commonly used in drink garnishes.

Drink rimmers count as garnishes, too, and can be made from salt or colored sugar. Add more flavor and flare by mixing ground lavender or chili powder in with the salt or sugar. To rim a glass, simply moisten the rim of the glass with a piece of fruit, syrup, or water, and dip it into a plate sprinkled with the powdered rimming ingredient.

Of course, there are also nonedible garnishes, such as little umbrellas, mini clothespins, picks or skewers (to hold chunks of fruit), and any other fun or elegant glass decorations to complement a special drink or party theme.

Don't forget the ice! By freezing berries or edible flowers into the ice cubes themselves, you can create floating drink decor. Go one step further by freezing fruit juice, tonic water, or tea in ice cube trays so they continue adding flavor to the drink as they melt.

EGGCELLENT TIPS

People are sometimes squeamish about using raw eggs in cocktails, but they have been incorporated into recipes dating back to the 1800s and give drinks rich texture. Egg whites give cocktails a silky quality and add a fluffy white cloud to the surface of the drink, while egg yolks make for a creamy, rich cocktail and so used in classic flips and nogs.

For those rightfully concerned about salmonella, be sure to wash the egg before cracking it open, as it is typically found on the shell rather than in the egg itself. And, of course, use eggs, dairy, or any food-based ingredient according to your own preference and judgment.

DRY SHAKE

When shaking an egg or cream into a cocktail, the mixture must first undergo a vigorous "dry" shake—i.e., *without* ice—to mix the ingredients and start to make the drink frothy and light. After the dry shake, add ice to the shaker and vigorously shake again before straining it into a glass.

SHAKE OR STIR?

A basic mixology rule is that if a drink is all liquor, it is stirred rather than shaken. Think: Manhattans, Negronis, Old Fashioneds, Martinis. In anticipation of anyone quoting James Bond famously requesting a Martini "shaken not stirred" in the 1964 movie *Goldfinger*, keep in mind that Bond had to ask for his drink to be shaken because a properly trained bartender would have stirred it. If the drink recipe calls for juice, cream, or egg, it is always shaken.

When shaking with ice, put enough ice into the shaker so that it is just poking out of the surface of the liquid, and then shake vigorously to both chill and slightly dilute the drink before straining into a chilled glass for a drink served *up* or over fresh ice for a drink served *on the rocks*. Avoid the temptation to "shake and dump"—sloshing the entire contents of a shaker into a glass, ice and all. We want to avoid this because the ice used for shaking is already melting quickly and you'll be left with a watery cocktail—yuck!

"Rolling" a drink is similar to shaking but much less vigorous. Pour the ice and liquid from one mixing glass or tin into another. This is repeated back and forth about five times. This technique is employed when someone wants to mix the ingredients well without watering the drink down too much by shaking.

If a drink has Champagne or another bubbly mixer, pour half of the bubbles into the glass, then shake and pour all the noncarbonated ingredients before topping off with more bubbles. This mixes the bubbly into the drink without losing carbonation.

MEASURING TIPS

1 barspoon = 1 teaspoon

The juice of ½ lime equals about ½ ounce.

The juice of ½ lemon equals about ¾ ounce.

When batching a drink for a larger quantity, simply translate ounces to cups and keep the same ratios in the recipe.

HOW DO YOU MEASURE LIQUOR?

As I am based in the United States, the recipes in this book are written in ounces. However, I'm aware that most other parts of the world use the metric system. If you're translating ounces to milliliters, keep in mind that one fluid ounce is equivalent to just under 30 milliliters. Based on this ratio, here is a quick reference guide:

½ ounce = 15 milliliters	2 ounces = 60 milliliters
¾ ounce = 20 milliliters	2½ ounces = 75 milliliters
1 ounce = 30 milliliters	3 ounces = 90 milliliters
1½ ounce = 45 milliliters	1 cup = 240 milliliters

> DOGS ARE NOT OUR WHOLE LIFE,
> BUT THEY MAKE OUR LIVES WHOLE.

—GEORGE BERNARD SHAW,
PLAYWRIGHT

CHAPTER
2

RESCUE ME!

WALK INTO ANY SHELTER AND YOU'LL SEE SOME POOR FUR-
ball cowering in a cage hoping to catch the eye of an adopter. Or maybe you have
crossed paths with a scraggly soul surviving on the streets, wondering how they
wound up alone and unloved. Homeless dogs may be scarred, scared, skittish,
skinny, and sad, but we instinctively know that, just like humans, rescue dogs
respond well when spoken to kindly and offered a gentle pat. When safely nes-
tled within a family, their emotional and physical transformations from mangy
mutts to beautiful canine companions prove that finding love has breathtaking
outcomes. Not to mention that daily walks (hello, workout partner!) and hanging
at home with our dog (hey, bestie!) enhance our own daily lives in ways we never
knew we needed. This chapter is an homage to the many homeless dogs in the

world, including some who have crossed my path and left an impression. I love discovering readers' stories of how they encountered their rescue dog and hope to hear more! As any adopter knows, once they are your very own, you'll find yourself wondering, "Exactly who rescued whom?"

HUG YOUR VET TODAY!

Next time you take your pup for a checkup, make a point of telling the tech and vet how much you appreciate them caring for your fur-babies. Veterinarians are animal lovers who deal with gut-wrenching situations every day yet keep showing up despite the toll on their mental and emotional health. I wrote my vet a sincere thank-you note after she took the time to console me after my beloved cat died suddenly. She later told me that she kept that note on a bulletin board above her desk and looked at it on the tough days. These folks are doing the work of angels, and we should let them know it with a kind word—or a bottle of bubbly.

SAY WHAT?

As you and your dog continue to get to know each other, there are several books to help you decipher your dog's communication. *Doggie Language* by Lili Chin features illustrations of canine body language for visual cues. *How Stella Learned to Talk* by Christina Hunger chronicles the speech pathologist's revolutionary word board created for her dog to be able to speak for herself by stepping on buttons that allow her to "say" words.

Stray Dog Sour

If any pup has an excuse to be a *sour*puss, it's one of the hundreds of millions of stray dogs worldwide. If you've seen a hungry dog searching a gutter for scraps of food or the terrified look of a dog abandoned at a shelter, it's hard to forget. We can help reduce the number of pets in shelters by funding spay and neuter programs in our communities and donating to organizations that offer low-cost sterilization. Every dog deserves to live in a safe environment with regular meals and a person to love. The most joyful wiggle in the world is from a dog who gets a sweet ending to their sour story. In the mixology world, a sour is one of the most versatile and popular drink formulas, and it is easy to customize to suit your taste: use two parts spirit (any alcohol), one part sweet (any syrup), and one part citrus (typically lemon or lime). This drink is a riff on a traditional Whiskey Sour, replacing the usual plain simple syrup with hibiscus flower syrup.

- 2 ounces Bourbon
- 1 ounce hibiscus flower syrup
  (see page 13 for syrup directions)
- 1 ounce freshly squeezed lemon juice
- Garnish: lemon wheel

Shake all ingredients with ice and strain into a cocktail glass to serve up, or over fresh ice in a rocks glass if you prefer your drinks on the rocks. Make a small slit in the peel of the lemon wheel and slide it onto the rim of the glass.

Brown-Eyed Girl

While volunteering as a dog walker at a local shelter, I came across a six-month-old puppy squished up against the side of her cage. Eyes downcast, she shrank as I approached. When I went home, I kept thinking about her. Each day for the next week, I returned to check on her, hoping she would find a great home, yet increasingly worried that her cage would be empty instead. Hoping to earn her trust, I climbed in her cage and sat quietly near her. When she finally mustered the courage to lean over and place a shy lick on my hand, my heart melted and I adopted her myself. Lula is my first dog "of my very own." As an adorable and lively retriever/Australian shepherd, she spent the first few months skidding across my new wood floors, herding the cats, gnawing the floorboards, and chewing the squeaker out of every toy. Now, years later, she still runs like black lightning at the dog park and barks invitations at everyone to play ball. I can no longer imagine waking up in a world without her exuberant tail wags as she trots out to bid "Good Morning!" to my menagerie of kitties, whether they like it or not. In honor of my brown-eyed girl, this chocolate version of my favorite Manhattan is tail-wagging-ly indulgent! To make a signature drink for your own pup, head to chapter 9 at the end of this book.

- 2 ounces Bourbon
- 1½ ounces chocolate liqueur
- ¾ ounce port
- Dash of chocolate bitters
- Garnish: chocolate-covered cherry

Stir all ingredients with ice in a mixing glass or cocktail shaker and strain into a cocktail glass. Plop the cherry into the glass or skewer several of them on a pick and lay it across the rim of the glass.

"

YOU CANNOT SHARE YOUR LIFE WITH A DOG
OR CAT AND NOT KNOW PERFECTLY WELL THAT ANIMALS
HAVE PERSONALITIES AND MINDS AND FEELINGS.

"

—DR. JANE GOODALL,
PRIMATOLOGIST AND ANTHROPOLOGIST

Blue Velvet

During the pandemic, my mom lost two dogs. First, her longtime companion Dinah succumbed to cancer. Her subsequent hospice foster, Charlie, was an emaciated senior cocker spaniel found wandering alone in the snowy Taos mountains. Thanks to my mom, he spent his last few months in spoiled-rotten comfort. After Charlie passed, my mom felt blue without a dog, but 2020 was an unusual year for adoptions. People who didn't have time to train a puppy in their pre-COVID-19 lives suddenly had long days with nothing to do. Stray animals reaped the benefit as adoption rates jumped from 58 percent to over 85 percent across the United States creating a shortage of available animals. Finally, in 2021, her name came up on the waiting list for a meet-and-greet with a three-month-old wiggle butt, who was so overcome with excitement that she peed down the shelter manager's shirt, then launched herself onto my dog Lula, who politely sidestepped the advance. Although blue heelers can be high spirited, they also learn quickly. And, this puppy's bright doggie smile and sunny personality were irresistible. Her white skin dusted with gray rain cloud splotches led to us naming her Ciela (a twist on the Spanish word *cielo* meaning "sky"). This drink honors blue heelers with its bluish color and a white fluffy cloud of whipped cream dotted with blueberries.

- 1 scoop vanilla ice cream
- ½ cup blueberries
- 2 ounces raspberry liqueur
- Garnish: A few blueberries and whipped cream

Blend the ice cream, blueberries, and liqueur in a blender for a couple of minutes, until it has a milkshake consistency. Then pour into a Collins glass and top with whipped cream and a few blueberries.

Tecate's Tale

In my 20s, I lived in a tiny studio in Venice Beach. So, when a boyfriend and I took a day trip to Tecate, Mexico, and found a very young puppy alone in a hot alley, I knew I couldn't keep her. But I also couldn't leave her. Her ribs pushed through her sparse, mud-crusted fur. And when her little Lab-mix face weakly lifted to mine, I promised those sad eyes we would get her to a better situation. Later that day, as our car approached the US border, the puppy shifted under the crumpled newspaper where I had hidden her in a box at my feet. I held my breath, hoping that she wouldn't reveal herself with a whimper. "Anything to declare?" asked the guard as we handed over identification. My boyfriend gave a wholesome smile and replied, "Oh, just a few souvenirs." The guard gestured toward me, "What's in there?" I nervously reached into the box and pulled out a small flowerpot—which I had been using as a dog bowl, sneaking tacos to the puppy until that very minute. Luckily, the guard was none the wiser and waved us through. Thirteen years later, an email from that long-since-ex boyfriend told me that Tecate had passed. He included a photo of her as an old dog wearing a birthday hat and anecdotes of their great life together. Although nowadays I'd highly recommend using a legal cross-border rescue, this drink is in honor of that happily-ever-after story. A twist on a traditional Michelada, it uses orange juice instead of tomato—the main ingredient, of course, is Mexican beer.

- ¾ ounce orange juice
- ½ ounce freshly squeezed lime juice
- 2 dashes Mexican hot sauce
- Salt and cayenne pepper, to taste
- 1 bottle (12 ounces) Mexican lager beer, chilled
- Garnish: Celery salt to rim glass

Rim a chilled Collins glass or bar mug with celery salt and pour in the juices, hot sauce, and seasonings. Then slowly add the beer and stir, gently, to mix.

Furever Friend

Bringing home an adorable puppy is the exciting start of a long journey for you both. Snuggles and Insta-worthy moments of cuteness are interspersed with house training, crate training, leash training, and puppy school, not to mention the inevitable chewed-up favorite shoes or expensive headphones. Getting to the other side of puppydom will require patience and consistency on your part, and of course, an adult rescue dog has their own challenges. You may be the first person your rescue dog trusts, and just like with any human, that will grow over time. The American Kennel Club has a wonderful quote on every page of its website that reaffirms the level of commitment we take on when we invite a canine companion into our lives. It starts with: "Owning a dog is not just a privilege; it's a responsibility . . ." Adoption is a promise to care for this dog until the end of its life. In return, your dog will protect you and love you like no other friend could. I, myself, try to live up to the

ACCENTUATE THE POSITIVE

Whether teaching a new puppy or an older rescue dog, patience and forgiveness will help them adjust to new surroundings and build trust with you. Expect a few accidents while they are learning, keeping in mind that the best training results come from praising good behavior rather than punishing mistakes. Positive Reinforcement Training is a specific method which encourages giving your dog a treat or toy when they do something good, optimizing their desire to please you. Kids can be great compassionate trainers, too! K9 Youth Alliance in Los Angeles teaches underserved youth volunteers how to train homeless dogs, which boosts the kids' self-esteem and makes the dogs more adoptable. Most importantly, do not punish your pup through fear or pain. The old-fashioned choke collars and electric shocks, or biting or stepping on dogs' paws, intimidating or smacking them are proven to be ineffective and downright abusive.

popular saying, "Be the person your dog thinks you are." I'll admit, it's not always easy . . . but she sure makes me want to try! Here is a sparkling drink to toast you and your four-legged BFF.

- 4 ounces sparkling wine
- 1 teaspoon grenadine
- Garnish: cherry

Pour the sparkling wine into a chilled Champagne flute or coupe or white wine glass. When the bubbles have settled, slowly drizzle in the grenadine so it sinks to the bottom of the glass, creating a layered effect. Drop in the cherry.

IN THE WHOLE HISTORY OF THE WORLD
THERE IS BUT ONE THING THAT MONEY CANNOT BUY...
TO WIT THE WAG OF A DOG'S TAIL.

—JOSH BILLINGS, WRITER

CHAPTER
3

WILL WORK FOR PATS

WE ALL KNOW THAT A DOG'S TRUE VALUE IS IN THEIR WAG-ging tail and loyal heart. Still, the physical abilities and personality traits of some of our canine buddies make them ideal working dogs, too. From herding cattle to sniffing out bombs to providing emotional support, some breeds are naturally inclined to go beyond the cuteness factor and make actual contributions to society. And let's not forget bar dogs. Many casual beachside bars or corner pubs have their own friendly dog whose job is to greet every regular as if they were coming home. Talk about a dream job for a social pup! This chapter celebrates those dogs who have found their mission in life and at the same time manage to make everyone else's life better.

The Racer

Cave drawings prove that the graceful greyhound has been treasured for millennia. Their elegant physiques and ability to chase fleet-footed wildlife across the desert also made them favorites of the pharaohs of Egypt, including Cleopatra. These dogs are even mentioned in the Bible, and their predecessors are believed to have traveled with Celtic tribes across Ireland, the British Isles, and modern-day Spain. Today, greyhounds are enjoying a resurgence in popularity as a household pet. Animal advocacy groups have successfully rendered dog racing illegal in most of the United States and help to place the retired dogs in loving homes where they can live their last years in comfort. In 1930, the classic Greyhound drink recipe first appeared in famed barman Harry Craddock's *Savoy Cocktail Book*. The original calls for gin, but in the 1950s the drink started to be made with vodka as well. Fun note: If you add a salt rim to the glass of a Greyhound, its name changes to a Salty Dog. In this twist, I've added lavender syrup into the drink and dried lavender flowers into the salt rim. Lavender and grapefruit are a heavenly combination and will take you straight over the finish line.

- 4 ounces freshly squeezed grapefruit juice
- 1½ ounces gin (or vodka)
- ¾ ounce lavender syrup
- Garnish: Grind 1 tablespoon dried culinary lavender flowers with 1 tablespoon Himalayan sea salt to make a tasty and aromatic rimmer

Moisten the rim of a cocktail glass by rubbing it with citrus fruit or water, then dip it into the lavender-salt mixture. Fill with ice and set aside. Shake the ingredients with ice. Gently strain into the ice-filled, rimmed glass.

DOGGIE DOCS

Numerous studies have shown that trained dogs can detect diseases through their keen sense of smell. They've been known to alert people to lung, breast, ovarian, bladder, and prostate cancers. There are even dogs who can sniff out COVID-19. Incredibly, many of these super-smeller dogs have a 99 percent success rate.

Mushie Slushie

The husky breed originated in chilly Siberia where they were family members to the nomadic Chukchi tribe. Huskies are strong, intelligent, and love to run, and their double coat of thick fur makes them suited to living and working in the snow. Despite being somewhat stubborn by nature, they are happiest when part of a pack, responding to a hearty "Mush!" from their human driver as they speed across the ice. When huskies were brought to Alaska in the early 1900s, dogsled racing for sport began, and sledding became a regular means of transportation for both people and goods. The most famous sled dog around that time was a fellow named Balto, who led a team of hero huskies through blizzard conditions to Nome with lifesaving antitoxin when a diphtheria outbreak ravaged the city in 1925, in what is known as the Serum Run. The famous Iditarod retraces some of that path as it follows a historic dogsled trade route from Anchorage to Nome. While some people love the tradition of the race, animal activists claim it is cruel to drive dogs so hard for human entertainment. Just like the tundra where huskies originated, this drink is served ice-cold and tastes minty fresh. The addition of rich chocolate liqueur gives a layered effect, like the beautiful, mottled coat of this fierce-yet-cuddly breed.

- 1½ ounces vodka
- 1 ounce white crème de menthe
- 2 ounces chocolate liqueur
- Garnish: fresh mint sprig

Fill a highball or Collins glass halfway with crushed ice, pour in the vodka and white crème de menthe, then stir to mix. Add the rest of the ice, then slowly add the chocolate liqueur, allowing it to create a layered effect. Tuck the mint sprig into the ice at the surface of the drink.

French Poodle 75

Whether the word *poodle* conjures a fluffy little floof with ribbons adorning its tiny curls or a hip-high, regal retriever, this breed's intelligence is second only to the border collie. They are equally skilled at performing useful tasks, serving as hunting companions, or wowing an audience as circus performers. Poodles are often referred to as "French," because they were thought to be descended from the Barbet water dog, a shaggy, curly-haired pooch. The French also consider the *caniche*, or poodle, their national dog. However, the poodle is more likely descended from a water dog in Germany called a *pudelhund*. Poodles are classified into three varieties according to size: standard, miniature, and toy, so their versatility—along with their lack of shedding—makes them one of the most adopted breeds worldwide and excellent service dogs. I chose the French 75 cocktail to honor this sturdy dog, as the drink is named for a French World War I firearm and it packs a punch. Many iterations of this drink exist, but it was likely created around 1915. My twist on this cocktail is adding some spicy ginger for a kick that might just make your hair curl.

SOMETIMES YOU DON'T NEED WORDS TO MAKE YOU FEEL BETTER. YOU JUST NEED THE NEARNESS OF YOUR DOG.

—NATALIE LLOYD, NOVELIST

- 3–4 ounces Champagne
- 1 ounce gin (or Cognac)
- ½ ounce fresh lemon juice
- 1 teaspoon freshly grated ginger
- ½ ounce simple syrup
- Garnish: lemon twist

Pour half of the Champagne into a chilled flute or coupe and set aside. Shake the gin, lemon juice, ginger, and simple syrup with ice, then strain into the glass. Fill with the remaining Champagne and lay the lemon twist across the rim of the glass.

Golden (Retriever) Cadillac

One look at a retriever puppy and it's easy to melt into a puddle of fawning goo. Their luscious fur and eager-to-please disposition make them a wonderful family dog. Originally, retrievers were bred as hunting dogs, specifically to find and carry back waterfowl to their humans, because their soft mouths kept the birds' bodies intact. There are six kinds of retrievers: Labrador, golden, Chesapeake Bay, flat coated, curly coated, and Nova Scotia Duck Tolling. Golden retrievers are among the most popular dog breeds, because they excel at obedience competitions, have a lot of energy (great for playing with children), and their curious minds keep them engaged with humans. The retriever needs both physical and mental exercise, so while going for a walk is fun for both of you, even a scenic drive helps to engage your dog's busy brain in constructive—rather than destructive— activities. The original Golden Cadillac cocktail dates back to the 1950s when a bartender in California supposedly created it for a young couple on their honeymoon road trip in just such a car. Perhaps not too many years later that same couple might have had a baby's car seat and a golden retriever of their own in the back of that shiny cruiser.

- 1 ounce vodka
- 1 ounce white crème de cacao
- 1 ounce heavy cream
- ¾ ounce Galliano botanical liqueur
- Garnish: grated chocolate

Shake all ingredients with ice and strain into a cocktail glass. Sprinkle the grated chocolate on the surface of the drink.

Loyal Hound

When a dog gets to do what its breed is best suited for, it experiences deep emotional satisfaction. The American foxhound was supposedly created and bred by George Washington for foxhunting, but hounds of all sorts have a natural talent for tracking. The Irish wolfhound was adept at killing large predators, including wolves. Beagles, bassets, dachshunds, and especially bloodhounds have an acute sense of smell, making them good at a range of scent-focused jobs. They also have stamina enough to run long distances after quick-moving prey or follow the scent of a missing person. These qualities have, historically, made them appealing for many jobs ranging from hunting excursions with British aristocracy to aiding detectives and search-and-rescue operations. But be warned, these dogs can become destructive if not given a chance to employ their inquisitive noses. Games such as hide-and-seek can be highly rewarding for these pups and bolster their emotional well-being. The classic drink Blood and Sand is one of my favorites and seems a fitting tribute for these hardworking hounds. It is strong, a bit unusual, and will leave you in search of another.

- ¾ ounce Scotch
- ¾ ounce sweet vermouth
- ¾ ounce cherry liqueur
- ¾ ounce orange juice
- Garnish: orange wheel

Shake all ingredients with ice. Pour over fresh ice into a double rocks glass. Place the orange wheel on the rim of the glass.

Rajapalayam Royale

The rare and ferocious Rajapalayam breed from Southern India was originally bred to hunt boar, and these dogs are said to be able to take down a tiger if their human is in danger. They can be a bit tricky as family pets as they are very energetic, headstrong, and highly protective of their owners, so they might appear aggressive to outsiders. A status symbol among Indian royalty, these clever canines were also incorporated into the army to help guard the borders. As warrior dogs in the Polygar and Carnatic wars against the British (around 1799–1805), they were fast, aggressive, and dedicated to their task. The Rajapalayam has been on the brink of extinction for decades, and there are currently efforts to revive this regal beast. The cocktail to pair with this breed needed to have a special ingredient, so I chose saffron from the crocus flower, which costs upwards of $5,000 per pound! Luckily, only a few strands are needed for the saffron syrup, and its beautiful color and aroma make this drink unique—just like this mysterious dog.

[THE RHODESIAN RIDGEBACK] WAS BRED TO HUNT LIONS . . . AND I CAN'T HELP BUT THINK THAT WAS A LITTLE BIT OF A SHOCK TO IT.

—RICKY GERVAIS, AWARD-WINNING ENTERTAINER AND ANIMAL ADVOCATE

- 3–4 ounces dry sparkling wine
- ½ ounce saffron syrup (see page 13 for syrup directions)
- Pinch of lime zest
- 1–2 dashes cardamom bitters
- Garnish: lime twist

Pour about half of the sparkling wine into a chilled Champagne flute or coupe. Add the syrup, lime zest, and cardamom bitters. Lightly stir to mix. Top with the remaining sparkling wine. Lay the lime twist across the rim of the glass.

Barry's Barrel

The Saint Bernard—the iconic working dog of Swiss origin—is often associated with a stiff drink due to the little booze barrel around its neck. But this is no party dog! These dogs were employed as mountain rescue professionals and guardians of the St. Bernard Hospice, founded in the 11th century as a place of worship and aid for travelers. Set within a dangerous mountain route between Italy and Switzerland, the Great St. Bernard Pass had been known for bandits. The Saint Bernard breed is descended from dogs gifted to the monks by noble families in the region for protection. Their fine reputation was furthered by the soldiers of Napoleon Bonaparte in the 1800s when they passed through the area. In 2005, the Barry Foundation took over the Saint Bernard breeding kennels from the monks, and its name came from a famous dog who rescued more than 40 people during his lifetime (1800–1814). There is even a museum called Barryland after him. May 28 is the annual Feast Day of the saint for whom the dogs are named—and a great excuse to celebrate these lifesaving pups. The liquor in those little barrels Saint Bernards carry was said to help revive people lost in the cold for many hours or even days. Some say they were filled with rum or brandy and others say local schnapps, so this recipe contains all of the above to please everyone, equally.

- ¾ ounce brandy
- ¾ ounce peach schnapps
- ¾ ounce rum
- ¾ ounce freshly squeezed lemon juice
- Garnish: cherry

Shake all ingredients with ice and strain into a chilled cocktail glass. Drop the cherry into the glass.

Firefall

Ask any kiddo which kind of dog hangs out at the fire station and they'll quickly identify a Dalmatian. We all know the black-and-white spotted canine as a fire-fighter mascot, but these dogs have played an important role in this profession dating back to the time of horse-drawn carriages. Due to their bravery, agility, and height, Dalmatians could run alongside horses, and their barking would both alert townspeople to the emergency and scare them out of the way of the clanging fire cart carrying water to blazes. The Dalmatian's origins are somewhat mysterious, but they are believed to come from an ancient race of dogs that can be traced back to the Dalmatia area in modern-day Croatia, as well as to the Greek island of Crete. Beloved by European aristocracy as far back as the 17th century because of their striking aesthetics, the tall dogs also protected their carriages and horses from human attackers and wild animals. The Dalmatians' good memory and striking black splotches made them equally appealing as entertainment dogs in traveling shows. This drink adds a bit of "fire" from the cinnamon and the black-and-white garnish is a nod to this breed's unique coat.

- 2 ounces cinnamon-flavored vodka
- 1½ ounces cream (or coconut creamer)
- ¾ ounce Maraschino cherry liqueur
- ½ ounce simple syrup infused with Red Hots (add a teaspoon of the candies to the water and sugar mixture while heating it)
- Garnish: tiny marshmallows and black licorice pieces on a skewer

Shake the ingredients with ice and strain into a cocktail glass. Lay the decorative black-and-white skewer on the rim of the glass.

THANK YOU FOR YOUR SERVICE

In 2021, a bipartisan law was passed in the United States requiring the Department of Veterans Affairs to provide service dogs to veterans suffering from post-traumatic stress disorder (PTSD). The Puppies Assisting Wounded Servicemembers (PAWS) for Veterans Therapy Act requires access to this proven method of assisting with the mental and physical pain suffered by people who have given so much to their country.

Badge of Honor

Did you know that in most countries harming a police dog carries the same punishment as harming a police officer? Ancient cultures in Persia, Greece, and Mesopotamia used dogs with their policing forces, and the first K9 officers in the United States went into action in New York City in 1907. These highly trained servants of the law are often raised from puppies to join the force, although some start out as shelter rescues or emotional and physical service dogs. The dogs live with their handlers when not on duty and stay with those families after they retire because their bond is so strong. Many of them are also bilingual (English and Spanish) and, once ready to start their jobs, are directed to bark to take their oath of office in an official ceremony. German shepherds and Belgian Malinois are among the most popular police dogs because they are incredibly smart and highly trainable. During their six- to nine-year career, they sniff out narcotics, participate in missing person searches, and sometimes physically take down a criminal on the run. Police dogs are so adept at identifying a target that they can even distinguish between identical twins—something that is far more difficult for humans to do with the naked eye. Did you know that most police uniforms around the world are blue? The (orange-flavored) blue curaçao liqueur gives this drink an indigo hue as a nod to the two- and four-legged officers who protect and serve our communities.

- 2 ounces pineapple juice
- 2 ounces coconut water
- 1 ounce tequila blanco
- ¾ ounce blue curaçao
- Garnish: pineapple wedge

Shake all ingredients with ice and strain into an ice-filled Collins glass. Make a slit in the pineapple wedge and slide it onto the rim of the glass.

Judy of the High Seas

Pointers' congenial personalities make them excellent service dogs even in terrible circumstances. Judy was a purebred English pointer and naval warship mascot in World War II. She survived the ship's bombing and wound up on a deserted island where she dug a hole to a potable freshwater spring, saving the marooned men's lives. The sailors and dog were soon forcibly removed to a Japanese prison camp on the island of Sumatra. There, aircraftsman Frank Williams shared his daily meager ration of rice with the starving dog and got her registered as an official canine prisoner of war, protecting her from being shot. Later, during their transport to another camp, their ship was torpedoed, so Williams dropped Judy into the sea. She then saved more men by bringing them debris to stay afloat and hauling others ashore. Williams and Judy helped each other survive until both returned to England where Judy was awarded the Dickin Medal from the People's Dispensary for Sick Animals (PDSA) in 1946: "For magnificent courage and endurance in Japanese prison camps, which helped to maintain morale among her fellow prisoners, and also for saving many lives through her intelligence and watchfulness." When Judy died, Williams buried her in a Royal Air Force coat and built her memorial. Today, her medal and collar can be found on display at the Imperial War Museum. This recipe calls for gin and tonic as both harken back to colonial times when British sailors mixed their daily gin ration with lime to fight scurvy and tonic as

BREAK THE CHAIN

In about half of the United States, it is illegal to keep dogs chained up day and night. Whether a household pet or a working security guard, dogs still need exercise and playtime to be emotionally, mentally, and physically healthy. You can help implement no-chain laws by reaching out to your local city councilmembers and state senators. A group of us in Santa Fe gathered signatures and attended city council meetings. This outreach and persistence successfully resulted in a no-chain law in our area. You can do the same!

a quinine to soothe stomach ailments. This maritime drink honors Judy who was not only a mascot but a working member of the Royal Navy.

- 1½ ounces gin
- ½ ounce freshly squeezed lime juice
- 4 ounces tonic
- Garnish: wedge of lime

Pour the gin, lime juice, and half the tonic into a highball glass and gently stir. Add the rest of the tonic and place the lime wedge on the rim of the glass.

ANIMALS ARE NOT BRETHREN, THEY ARE NOT UNDERLINGS;
THEY ARE OTHER NATIONS CAUGHT WITH OURSELVES
IN THE NET OF LIFE AND TIME.

—HENRY BESTON,
AUTHOR AND NATURALIST

CHAPTER 1

A WALK ON THE WILD SIDE

GENETICALLY SPEAKING, WILD DOGS ARE JUST ONE STEP away from the companions we know and love in our own homes. In fact, our own pets share DNA with the canids who, even before humans stood upright, had already been evolving over several millions of years. Way back in their early forms, some wolflike creatures grew as big as bears! Today, indigenous canines are found on every continent except Antarctica. Some of our ancient cultures tell stories of their fierceness and cunning, while others include wild dogs among their spiritual guides and friends of the gods. How we relate to them depends upon whether we choose to observe them fearfully or with reverence. And, just like most wildlife, they would rather avoid interacting with us even more than we would want to avoid them. The untamed canines that wander through the magical forests, marshes, rain forests, and savannas across the globe are part of the larger inextricably inter-twined ecosystem, and thus their survival is tied to our own. Reading through the fascinating wild dogs in this chapter, you may recognize similarities in your own furry friend as all domesticated breeds today are descended from them.

KILLING CONTESTS BACKFIRE

To animal lovers, it's hard to believe that wildlife-killing contests are legal in more than 40 US states. These sport hunters often, perhaps unknowingly, kill endangered wild dog species along the way. And, when they kill the leader of a wolf pack, they disrupt family group-ings. This perpetuates destructive cycles because it can result in hun-gry orphaned pups looking for food on farms and in urbanized areas, which is often what prompted these sprees in the first place. Protecting forested areas, and the animals within them, keeps them happily living there rather than venturing into human settlements.

WHEN THE MAN WAKED UP HE SAID, "WHAT IS WILD DOG DOING HERE?" AND THE WOMAN SAID, "HIS NAME IS NOT WILD DOG ANY MORE, BUT THE FIRST FRIEND, BECAUSE HE WILL BE OUR FRIEND FOR ALWAYS AND ALWAYS AND ALWAYS."

—RUDYARD KIPLING,
BEST-SELLING AUTHOR OF *THE JUNGLE BOOK*

Leader of the Pack

The majestic wolf is perhaps the most iconic wild dog featured in myths and legends across several continents and many centuries. Wolves are the most direct ancestors of today's domesticated dogs. These highly social animals live in packs of five to eight members and, as adept predators, help to maintain the circle of life in the forests and mountains. When they feast on other large animals, such as deer, the carcasses they leave behind become "doggie bags" for insects, scavenger birds, and even bears. In fact, wolves' contribution to natural ecosystems has been spotlighted in recent years due to the Yellowstone Wolf Project, a detailed study spanning the 25 years since wolves were reintroduced into the national park. By 1920, the US government had eradicated wolves from the park in an effort to "tame" it. But the absence of these carnivores threw wildlife and vegetation off-balance. In 1995, wolves from Canada and Montana were brought back into Yellowstone to reclaim their crucial role in the park's ecological processes, as documented in the study. Across the United States today, the Alaskan gray wolf is off the endangered species list, but the Mexican gray wolf—a smaller breed living in Mexico and the southwestern states—has been all but eliminated in the wild. Clearly, we all still have a lot of work to do to protect these canines and their habitats. This cocktail pays respect to the great work at Yellowstone and their leadership in wildlife conservation.

- 2 ounces vodka
- ¾ ounce yellow Chartreuse
- ½ ounce dry vermouth
- Dash of bitters
- Garnish: lemon twist

Stir all ingredients with ice and strain into a chilled cocktail glass. Lay the lemon twist on the rim of the glass or drop it in.

Tippling Trickster

Coyotes are adaptable and clever, making the Looney Tunes cartoon character Wile E. Coyote an appropriate anthropomorphism. More fun facts about these agile canines: they can run over 40 miles per hour, jump a span of 12 feet, and are excellent swimmers. In some Native American groups, the coyote is known as a mischievous trickster and featured prominently in children's stories. The word *coyote* originates from the Aztec word *coyotl*, and these wild dogs are prominent figures in many ancient North American myths. Aside from being cunning, they are also often portrayed as beneficial to society, depending on the perspective of the story. Some indigenous legends depict the coyote as a companion to the Great Creator at the beginning of time, using his high-pitched howl to sing other beasts into creation. A well-known Secwepemc story is called "Coyote Brings Food from the Upper World." Like the story, this cocktail includes corn and berries, which grow wild in North America.

HOW CAN WE EXPECT WILD ANIMALS TO SURVIVE IF WE GIVE THEM NOWHERE IN THE WILD TO LIVE?

—ANTHONY DOUGLAS WILLIAMS,
WRITER AND ANIMAL ACTIVIST

- 8–10 raspberries (about 2 tablespoons)
- 3 ounces corn milk (blend corn kernels into a puree, press through a sieve, and collect the milky liquid)
- 1½ ounces Bourbon
- ½ ounce agave nectar
- Garnish: 3–5 raspberries on a toothpick or skewer

Muddle the raspberries in the bottom of a cocktail shaker, holding back a few for the garnish. Add the other ingredients and shake with ice. Strain into a cocktail glass, and place the raspberry skewer on the rim of the glass.

Dingo Baby

Dingoes were likely brought to Australia by Southeast Pacific people as companion animals thousands of years ago. Over time, most returned to the wild, although some remained within Aboriginal tribal communities. Still, many modern-day breeds such as the Australian cattle dog and kelpies have ancient dingo genetics visible in their compact body size, alert minds, and strong bond with their human. Rather than bark, dingoes give a sort of yowl when communicating, as do some of the domesticated dogs to whom they are related. Fun aside: Did you know that in Australia, sometimes donkeys are used to patrol farm boundaries and are known to literally *kick* out wild dogs sneaking in to hunt the sheep? Many Americans first heard about dingoes from the 1980 Australian murder trial where an accused woman defended herself by claiming, "A dingo ate my baby!" Versions of this phrase were irresistible to comedy writers stateside, and this was spoofed on a famed *Seinfeld* episode where the character Elaine exclaims, "Maybe the dingo ate your baby!" Similar lines have been used on *The Simpsons, Alf, Frasier, Family Guy*, and *Two and a Half Men*. For a time in pop culture, it became hard to even say "dingo" without attaching it to a baby reference—hence this wine-based drink, which uses Australian Shiraz as a base.

- 1 medium sprig fresh sage (pluck 6 leaves for muddling)
- 1 tablespoon sour cherry jam or puree
- 4 ounces Australian Shiraz
- Garnish: the top part of the sage sprig

Muddle the plucked sage leaves and jam in the bottom of a cocktail shaker. Add the wine and shake with ice. Strain into an ice-filled red wine glass. Double strain the liquid through a sieve if you do not want any pieces of muddled sage in the drink. Place the top of the sage sprig on the rim of the glass, then fasten it with a mini drink garnish clip or tuck it into the ice.

ShoLoRita

The xoloitzcuintli, or xolo ("sho-lo") for short, is one of the most ancient dog breeds, tracing back to Aztec culture. Although sometimes called the Mexican hairless dog, they do have very short hair. Their name comes from the Aztec god of the underworld called Xolotl combined with *itzcuintli*, the Aztec word for "dog." These prized animals were seen as guardians and believed to ward off both physical intruders and evil spirits. Some saw them as having healing properties because without as much hair their skin radiated more heat than other dogs, which could comfort and give lifesaving warmth when they lay alongside someone who was ill. Those that have been domesticated are said to be affectionate and strongly bonded to their human family. Xolos were popular in the 1930s and '40s, and artists such as Frida Kahlo and Diego Rivera portrayed the breed in their art. The xolo population has dwindled in the wild and captivity, but they are starting to have a bit of a resurgence. Their rarity makes them a status symbol as a wild-dog-turned-pet. This drink features a smoky mezcal and is a bit wild in nature in honor of this unique breed.

I THINK SOMETIMES WE NEED TO TAKE A STEP BACK AND JUST REMEMBER WE HAVE NO GREATER RIGHT TO BE HERE THAN ANY OTHER ANIMAL.

—DAVID ATTENBOROUGH,
AUTHOR AND NATURAL HISTORIAN

- 1½ ounces mezcal
- ¾ ounce tamarind puree
- ½ ounce freshly squeezed lime juice
- ½ ounce agave nectar
- Garnish: lime wheel

Shake all ingredients with ice and strain over fresh ice in a rocks glass. Place the lime wheel on the rim of the glass.

Silver Foxed Vixen

Foxes don't typically pose a threat to domesticated pets—their main diet is rodents and, perhaps, the occasional chicken, which is how they tend to get a bad reputation. Foxes, however, are integral to controlling the rabbit population, which can prove even more troublesome to anyone trying to grow produce. Did you know that these wild dogs are extremely playful and are sometimes compared more to cats than dogs because, like felines, they have retractable claws, vertical pupils, and whiskers on their faces? Foxes come in a variety of colors. Gray or silver foxes are commonly found in North America, and in England they are mostly red, though the occasional rare melanic black or white one makes an appearance. During the 18th century, when the Industrial Revolution was going on in England, roads and railways cut across private land, making it harder for the aristocratic landowners to hunt large forest animals, such as deer. Sadly, this is when hunting hares and foxes really took off. Nowadays, though, just as bullfighting has been outlawed in much of the world, cruel foxhunting has become illegal in many places due to its barbaric methods of chasing down the animals and dwindling fox populations. A male fox is called a *dog fox* and the female a *vixen*, while the term *silver fox* is slang for an attractive middle-aged man, although Marvel comics give the name to a female character who is Wolverine's sly lover. Sultry and sophisticated—like the slinky animal—this drink features a gin base as an homage to England finally outlawing foxhunting in 2004.

- 1½ ounces London Dry gin
- ¾ ounce freshly squeezed lemon juice
- ¾ ounce honey syrup (see page 13 for syrup directions)
- 1 egg white
- Garnish: powdered sugar

Rim a cocktail glass with powdered sugar, then set aside. Shake all ingredients with ice and pour into the rimmed glass.

Anubis Reviver

Jackals are a unique mishmash of other wild dogs. They are a bit smaller than wolves, have the small face and fluffy tail of a fox, and the long, alert ears of a German shepherd and its wolf predecessor. They are omnivorous scavengers who consume everything from wild berries to gazelles and reptiles, according to the season and what they encounter. These wild dogs can live up to 16 years and have strong familial bonds, often hunting in pairs. There are three species of jackal: The black-backed prefers woodlands and is most common in South Africa, Namibia, Kenya, and Somalia. The golden jackal prefers deserts, savannas, and grasslands in places such as North Africa, Southern Asia, and southeastern Europe, primarily Greece, Romania, Italy, and Bulgaria. And the side-striped jackal lives in a wetter environment such as tropical Africa. In Egyptian culture, the jackal is associated with the god of death, Anubis. Jackals likely got that association because they sometimes scavenged for human remains in cemeteries. This cocktail is inspired by the original version of the classic Corpse Reviver. The drink's later version, called a Corpse Reviver No. 2, is made with gin and a white fortified wine.

- 1 ounce Cognac
- ¾ ounce sweet vermouth
- ¾ ounce Calvados (French apple brandy)
- ¾ ounce freshly squeezed lemon juice
- ¼ ounce absinthe
- Garnish: lemon twist

Shake all ingredients with ice and strain into a cocktail glass. Place the lemon twist on the rim of the glass or drop it into the drink.

Giggle Water

Hyenas are considered funny little guys, often misrepresented as lowly scavengers skulking around rotting carcasses or picking over the bones of a lion's kill in sub-Saharan Africa. Surprisingly, though, that depiction has it backward. Hyenas' speed and endurance allow them to chase and take down large beasts, such as water buffalos, making them even more successful predators than big cats. Their incredibly powerful jaw muscles allow them to apply tremendous force and easily crack open bones measuring two inches in diameter. Sadly, these ferocious hunters are also known to rid their territory of lion cubs because they could potentially grow into rivals. Born with teeth intact, eyes open, and ready to prowl, these wild dogs are unlike the usual helpless mammal babies. Hyena family groupings are matriarchal and called clans rather than packs, often including 120 members or more. Hyenas' intelligence rivals that of chimpanzees, and their 20-year life span makes them one of the longest living wild species of canine. The famous hyena "laugh" is not an expression of happiness, but rather anxiety. They also make a whooping howl as a form of long-distance communication—the sound can travel up to three miles. This rich cocktail is a wild tipple much like the hyena itself—light, strong, and possibly stirring up a giggle or two.

FARM-TO-DOG DISH

In the wild, dogs eat mammals, insects, birds, and fish—basically whatever they can catch or scavenge. At times, they survive on plants, rotting fruit, grasses, and even excrement from other animals. (Mystery solved as to why pet dogs love "snacks" from the kitty litter box!) I love cooking for all my friends, including my dogs, and have found that when I boil meat with sweet potatoes and carrots, then add raw eggs (with shells) to the mixture, and blend it all until smooth, my dogs' coats get incredibly shiny. I just dollop a couple of tablespoons over their dry food. Of course, before changing your own dog's diet, consult their vet.

- 2 ounces coconut water
- 1½ ounces cachaça (or white rum)
- ¾ ounce fig liqueur
- Garnish: fresh fig (green or purple)

Shake all ingredients with ice and strain into a cocktail glass. Slice the fresh fig to sit on the rim of the glass.

> DOGS ARE OUR LINK TO PARADISE.
> THEY DON'T KNOW EVIL OR JEALOUSY OR DISCONTENT.
> TO SIT WITH A DOG ON A HILLSIDE ON A GLORIOUS
> AFTERNOON IS TO BE BACK IN EDEN, WHERE DOING
> NOTHING WAS NOT BORING . . . IT WAS PEACE.

—MILAN KUNDERA,
AWARD-WINNING PLAYWRIGHT AND AUTHOR OF
THE UNBEARABLE LIGHTNESS OF BEING

SHOW, DON'T TELL

One of the rules of great storytelling is to let the reader or viewer *see* the story unfold rather than explaining every detail to them. Dogs interpret our interactions in much the same way. Tone of voice helps convey if you are pleased or frustrated, but just like young children, their vocabulary is limited. So, dogs interpret a lot from your facial expression. If your face lights up when you say "good morning" to your dog, their face will also brighten. If you are weary, bored, or upset, your dog will also likely feel uneasy and worry that they did something to provoke your bad mood. Try an experiment with your pup and greet them with a happy, friendly expression and higher-pitched positive words and see their whole body electrify with joy. Even if they don't understand the verbiage, your body language will convey everything they need to know.

5

FAMOUS FURBABIES

THE ACTOR W.C. FIELDS FAMOUSLY SAID, "NEVER WORK WITH children or animals," because no matter how talented an actor may be, the animal is sure to steal the spotlight. We are fascinated by other species' abilities to learn tricks, play along in imaginary circumstances, and display emotion just like a human actor does. In literature and entertainment, writers sometimes anthropomorphize dogs, giving us a glimpse into what they might think or say if they spoke a human language. Dogs in movies, books, and TV shows have made us laugh, cry, and fall in love with them. How many times have you cheered a doggie hero in a movie, laughed along with your favorite cartoon pup, or shed a tear while reading a book about the bond between a dog and their human? Through entertainment, we get to explore what our own dog would say or do if given the opportunity to take center stage and relate to them even more than we already do.

Snoopy's Red Baron

Peanuts creator and cartoonist Charles Schulz declared that "Happiness is a warm puppy"—and dog lovers agree. A snuggly pup and their hilarious antics bring a smile to anyone's face, and we can't help but wonder what they are thinking. Viewers get a peek inside the mind of Charlie Brown's feisty beagle Snoopy whenever he jumps on top of his doghouse and fantasizes about being a World War I pilot going after the Red Baron. In fact, the real Red Baron was Manfred von Richthofen, a German pilot in that war and one of the most famous aviators in history. Snoopy fans flock to the Charles M. Schulz Museum in Santa Rosa, California, to learn more about the artist and his work through the various exhibits. Meanwhile, the Snoopy Museum in Tokyo features a Peanuts Café where guests drink and dine surrounded by their favorite characters and enjoy a special party on Snoopy's birthday, August 10. This liquid homage has a fiery taste in honor of Snoopy's wish to take the Baron down in flames.

- 1½ ounces cinnamon-flavored vodka
- ¾ ounce freshly squeezed lemon juice
- ½ ounce grenadine
- Garnish: powdered sugar rim

Rim a cocktail glass with powdered sugar and set aside. Shake all ingredients with ice and gently strain into the glass.

Ring My Bell

A female Chihuahua named Gidget found fame in 1990s TV ads where she appeared wearing a sombrero and saying, "*Yo quiero Taco Bell!*" Latino and Hispanic advocacy groups protested the commercials' cultural stereotyping, and they were eventually—and rightfully—discontinued. However, Gidget, the dog actor, continued her showbiz career in national commercials and as Bruiser's mom in *Legally Blonde 2: Red, White & Blonde.* To honor this doggie starlet, and the Mexican state after which Chihuahuas are named, this drink features mezcal with a dash of spice, orange juice, and cinnamon. And, to *chime* in with a little liquor knowledge: Did you know that mezcal is the spirits category for all agave spirits? Tequila is actually a kind of mezcal made specifically from the Blue Weber agave plant. Other kinds of mezcal come from other agave plants such as Tobala and Raicilla. Experiment by tasting various mezcals when you have the opportunity so you can pick your favorite for this recipe.

- 2 ounces freshly squeezed orange juice
- 1½ ounces mezcal
- ½ ounce freshly squeezed lime juice
- ½ ounce cinnamon syrup (see page 13 for syrup directions)
- Garnish: cinnamon stick

Shake all ingredients with ice and strain into a cocktail glass, or strain over fresh ice in a rocks glass. Garnish with the cinnamon stick.

Bruiser's Cosmo

Could we really imagine Elle Woods, the central character in the film *Legally Blond*, without her little rescue Chihuahua? More than a favorite accessory to her permanently pink wardrobe, Bruiser is Elle's best friend as she tries to prove that she can, indeed, successfully navigate law school. The dog actor, named Moonie, was trained by Hollywood dog handler Sue Chipperton, who also helped train Gidget from the Taco Bell commercials. A nod to Elle's favorite color, the Cosmopolitan is the perfect pink drink to pair with this celebrity dog as we can easily imagine Elle enjoying one herself. This variation substitutes cherry liqueur for the Cosmo's traditional orange liqueur, a fresh take on an old classic which seems fitting for the brainy beauty and her pup.

- 1½ ounces citrus-flavored vodka
- ¾ ounce cherry liqueur
- ¾ ounce freshly squeezed lime juice
- ½ ounce cranberry juice
- Garnish: lime wheel

Shake all ingredients with ice and strain into a Martini glass. Place the lime wheel on the rim of the glass.

WHAT'S IN A NAME

Some dog names are so ingrained in American pop culture that they seem cliché, yet have interesting origins. For example, the phrase "See Spot run!" was popularized by the Dick and Jane book series, which helped kids learn to read from the 1930s to the '70s as Gen Xers and those older may remember. And, going back even further, this name has associations with the three-headed monstrous dog Cerberus of Greek myth with roots in Sanskrit from the word *Kerberos*, which means "spotted." The common name Fido came from President Abraham Lincoln's dog. He gave him that name as a derivative of *fides* in Latin meaning "faith" or "faithful." His dog's popularity made the name catch on to such an extent that it is almost synonymous with a canine companion.

The Squirrel of Dug's Dreams

Dug's goofy demeanor and desire to please make him an exemplary adventure companion in Pixar's *Up*, a heartwarming emotion tickler. However, despite his strongest efforts to listen and follow commands, Dug cannot refrain from being distracted anytime a squirrel runs by. All his doggie instincts go on high alert as his head snaps toward the movement and he blurts out, "Squirrel!" The catchphrase became part of pop culture vernacular and is jokingly used whenever someone is suddenly distracted. The natural choice to honor this cartoon dog is the Pink Squirrel, invented during the 1940s at Bryant's Cocktail Lounge in Milwaukee. This drink is made with crème de noyaux, a bright pink nutty and herbaceous liqueur popularized in the 19th century. Originally, its color was derived from the cochineal, an insect used for dyeing food and drinks, including some popular bitter Italian liqueurs.

- 1½ ounces crème de noyaux
- 1½ ounces white crème de cacao
- 1½ ounces heavy cream
- Garnish: freshly grated nutmeg

Shake all ingredients vigorously, then strain into a cocktail glass. Grate the nutmeg over the surface of the drink.

Faithful Friend

In Homer's classic the *Odyssey*, our hearts ache to read about Odysseus's faithful companion Argos. From puppyhood, he had been a prized hunting dog and was included as a member of the family; in fact, he was Odysseus's favorite. However, when Odysseus departed for Troy, Argos was left behind. The once noble dog was soon neglected, covered in fleas, and forced to sleep on piles of dung. The story goes that the heartbroken dog hung on for 20 years, waiting to see his human again. After Odysseus survived a shipwreck and other adventures, he finally made his way back to Ithaca. Once there, he disguised himself by wearing ragged clothes and snuck back into his own palace, which had been overrun with traitors. Unlike the humans who were easily fooled, his dog knew him immediately. Argos, now old and weak, willfully mustered all his strength to greet his human, wagging his tail with joy. His life's deepest wish fulfilled, Argos died moments after the encounter. That kind of love and loyalty is the stuff doggie legends are made of, and this tale demonstrates that our special bond with dogs is as ancient as the great civilizations of humanity. This drink features Greek mastiha made from the resin of the skinos tree, which grows on the island of Chios, and whose sap is believed to have healing properties. It has a woodsy and somewhat botanical taste reminiscent of fennel, anise, and mint.

- 2 tablespoons cucumber, peeled, seeded, and diced
- 2 ounces mastiha liqueur
- 1½ ounces chamomile tea
- ¾ ounce freshly squeezed lemon juice
- Garnish: skewer of feta cheese and Greek olives

Muddle the cucumber in the bottom of a mixing glass. Add the mastiha, tea, and lemon juice. Shake with ice and strain into a cocktail glass. Place the garnish skewer on the rim of the glass.

Scooby Snax

This crime-fighting scaredy-dog has won the hearts of children and adults the world over since September 13, 1969. In each episode, Scooby—a timid Great Dane—joined his human pals in chasing bad guys and bumbled his way through a string of silly antics until they saved the day. Fun fact: Scooby's original voice actor, Don Messick, was also the voice for Astro, the family dog on *The Jetsons,* a futuristic cartoon of the same era. *Scooby-Doo* has been rebooted several times over the last half-century, and in later years, Scooby was joined by a canine sidekick named Scrappy. In addition to the inner satisfaction that comes from fighting crime and solving mysteries, Scooby's valor was motivated by dog treats called Scooby Snacks. The ingredients that made these canine yummies so irresistible were never revealed in the cartoon but, in an interview, producer William Hanna said that he imagined they would taste like a caramel-flavored cookie, so his description is the inspiration for this drink.

- 2 ounces vanilla vodka
- 1 ounce caramel-flavored syrup
- 1 ounce heavy cream (or coconut cream for dairy-free)
- Garnish: ground graham cracker crumbs

Moisten the rim of a cocktail glass or rocks glass and dip it in the graham cracker crumbs, then set aside. Shake all ingredients with ice and gently strain the mixture into the glass.

Dry Humpin' Martini

Brian Griffin is one of the main protagonists on the popular animated series *Family Guy*. He speaks French, loves opera and jazz, writes for the *New York Times*, and loves dry Martinis. In between spouting witticisms and vulgarities, he goes to therapy and works on a novel. Did I mention this amusing character is the family's rescue Lab? Voiced by show creator and actor Seth MacFarlane, Brian sneers at his numbskull humans, and when utterly exasperated, he is known to ask, "*Who do you have to hump to get a dry Martini around here?*" which makes for an easy cocktail choice to pair with this snooty celebrity pup. The original Martini was created in the early 1900s with gin, a hefty amount of vermouth, and a dash of orange bitters. Vodka was not popularized in cocktail culture until the 1950s, which is when the Vodka Martini appeared. Asking for a "dry" Martini indicates to the bartender that you prefer little, if any, dry vermouth in it. People not familiar with vermouth or bitters sometimes leave them out entirely, resulting in mere ice-shaken vodka passing for the iconic drink. Keep in mind that without any vermouth at all, it's not even a Martini. As explained earlier on page 16, drinks that contain all liquor should be stirred.

SOME OF MY BEST LEADING MEN HAVE BEEN DOGS AND HORSES.

—ELIZABETH TAYLOR, ACTRESS

- 2½ ounces vodka
- ¼ ounce dry vermouth
- Dash of orange bitters
- Garnish: lemon twist

Stir all ingredients with ice and strain into a chilled cocktail glass. Place the twist on the rim of the glass or drop it into the drink.

Arigatou Akamaru

This faithful dog of Japanese anime is a skilled ninja, who was entrusted to his human Kiba when he was a puppy. The white Great Pyrenees eventually grows big enough for Kiba to ride on his back, and they undertake warrior missions together. When Akamaru goes into ninja mode, he often turns red, which is reflected in his name: *aka* means "red" and *maru* means "circle" or "perfection" and is a common ending for male names in Japan. He can also activate a special beast human clone technique they developed together, so he can also take on his human's appearance when fighting. This cocktail is a unique and delicious sipper with Japanese sake as the base, perfect to accompany our own daydreams of sharing wild adventures with our dogs.

- 4–6 shiso leaves (also called perilla leaves and found in Asian markets and gourmet food stores)
- 1 ounce plum wine
- 3 ounces sake
- ½ ounce lemon soda
- Garnish: mochi candies on a toothpick

Muddle the shiso leaves in the bottom of a mixing glass to crush them slightly, releasing aroma and flavor. Add the plum wine, sake, and lemon soda and shake with ice. Strain over fresh ice in a Collins glass and place the garnish across the rim.

Ruby Slipper

Our dogs would happily accompany us to the ends of the Earth and beyond, as seen in the classic film *The Wizard of Oz*. Having Toto by her side reassured Dorothy that she could navigate a strange new dangerous world, even with the Wicked Witch of the West on her tail. In real life, the doggie actor portraying Toto was actually a female terrier named Terry. One of the most prolific movie star dogs of all time, she appeared in 16 films. In addition to working with Judy Garland, Terry was also in two films with child actor Shirley Temple. This drink is named after the magical shoes Dorothy clicks together to transport herself—and Toto, too—out of the fantastical land of Oz by reciting, "There's no place like home." Incidentally, there were four pairs of shoes created for the film, and the only set available for public viewing is on display at the National Museum of American History in Washington, DC.

SUCH SHORT LITTLE LIVES OUR PETS HAVE TO SPEND
WITH US, AND THEY SPEND MOST OF IT WAITING
FOR US TO COME HOME EACH DAY.

—JOHN GROGAN,
BEST-SELLING AUTHOR OF *MARLEY AND ME*

- 1½ ounces cherry vodka
- ¾ ounce poppy liqueur (or substitute with elderflower liqueur)
- ½ ounce freshly squeezed lime juice
- Splash of ruby red grapefruit juice
- Garnish: cherry (fresh or Maraschino)

Shake all ingredients with ice and strain into a cocktail glass. Drop the cherry into the drink.

Hard Knock Highball

The story of Little Orphan Annie captured the hearts of audiences across several mediums and generations. It originated as a comic strip in 1924, became a radio show in 1931, opened on Broadway as a musical in 1977 and, in 1982, was released as a feature film. Obviously, over that time span, multiple actors have been cast to play both Annie and her dog, Sandy. The original Sandy in the Broadway show also appeared in the film. He was a beige terrier mix adopted from the Connecticut Humane Society who had been abused as a puppy and was scheduled for euthanasia on the day he was adopted. The grateful pup seized his second chance at life and went on to play Sandy for 2,377 stage performances until the show closed in 1983. He also appeared twice at the Tony Awards and visited Presidents Jimmy Carter and Ronald Reagan at the White House. This pooch started out with a "hard knock life" and retired with a Hollywood ending, so this drink is sweet, sour, and certainly celebratory. The story is set during the Great Depression, which followed on the heels of Prohibition (1920–1933), so this gin drink is also a nod to the "bathtub gin" people were illegally making at home during those bleak years.

- 1½ ounces gin
- ¾ ounce orange liqueur
- ¾ ounce freshly squeezed lemon juice
- ¾ ounce freshly squeezed orange juice
- Champagne, to top
- Garnish: orange wheel

Shake all ingredients (except the Champagne) with ice and strain into a tall ice-filled red wine glass. Top with the Champagne. Stir lightly and garnish with the orange wheel.

My Best Pal

"Lassie Come Home" was a short story by Eric Knight published in the *Saturday Evening Post* in 1938 inspired by his own collie named Toots. It moved the hearts of so many readers that he turned it into a novella, selling over a million copies in 1939. Metro-Goldwyn-Mayer (MGM) then bought the theatrical rights, and in 1940, a dog named Pal was cast in the title role. The original story was about an impoverished family in Yorkshire, England. The father sells his son's beautiful dog to a Scottish duke, but the dog loves the boy so much that he escapes and finds his way home. In 1954, Lassie debuted in a television series set in California, and the starring role was then played by Pal's own son who, with professional foresight, had been given the name Lassie. In 1978, the final *Lassie* film was made with Pal's sixth-generation descendant. In honor of the original version of the story, this drink is made with Scotch as a base and hearty apple cider.

- 1½ ounces Scotch
- ½ ounce honey syrup (see page 13 for syrup instructions)
- 3 ounces apple cider
- Dash of rhubarb bitters (if not available, any bitters will work)
- Garnish: apple slice dusted with ground cinnamon

Stir to mix the Scotch and honey syrup in the bottom of a tall glass or bar mug. Add the cider and fill with ice. Dash the bitters on top and garnish with the apple slice.

TAKE A BITE OUTTA WASHINGTON

President Joe Biden's dog Major is the first shelter dog to live in the White House and the first dog to have had an In*dog*uration a few days before his human was sworn in to be the 46th president of the United States. Over 10,000 people tuned in (I was one of them!), and the $10 tickets for online viewing benefited the Delaware Humane Association where the president and his wife, Dr. Jill Biden, adopted him in 2018. Like most of us in an overwhelming situation, Major had a few "growing pains" during his first year in Washington and nipped a security guard—or two. So, he went to live with family friends to avoid any further debacles. The public can follow the ongoing adventures of dogs in the White House on Instagram at @FirstFamilyDogs and see what they are up to in the Oval *Paw*ffice.

6

DOGS RULE

FROM THE LOWLIEST TO THE MIGHTIEST AMONG US, EVERY
human knows that their dog will always be by their side, no matter how many
challenges may be lurking in the shadows of our private or public lives. In the
backbiting world of politics, leaders find refuge from the public eye at home, where
partners, children, and close friends can provide a safe haven from the otherwise
constant scrutiny. But the love of a dog is like no other, so it is not surprising that
many world leaders publicly demonstrate how much their dogs mean to them. The
famous furbabies in this chapter are about as intriguing as the people themselves.

Pushinka's Purpose

Did a pup help end the Cold War? While president, John Kennedy's dog, Pushinka—Russian for *fluffy*—became famous for three main reasons: Her mother was the first dog to fly into space and return safely. She was accused of being a Russian puppy spy. And she helped save the world from nuclear destruction! It all began at a state dinner when First Lady Jackie Kennedy had a lively conversation with Soviet leader Nikita Khrushchev about his famous space dogs, Belka and Strelka, who had orbited Earth the year before. A few months later, one of Strelka's puppies arrived at the White House as a gift. This gesture is believed by many to have helped warm international relations between the two superpowers. It is said that President Kennedy enjoyed a Bloody Mary, so I'm suggesting that you make this one with Russian vodka and raise a glass to world peace.

- 3 ounces tomato juice
- 1½ ounces vodka
- ¾ ounce fresh lemon juice
- 1 teaspoon horseradish, or to taste
- Dash of Worcestershire sauce
- Dash of hot sauce
- Freshly ground pepper, to taste
- Celery salt, to taste
- Garnish: celery, pickles, olives, or your favorite Bloody Mary garnish

Roll all ingredients with ice (see page 16) and serve in a chilled Collins glass or bar mug. Garnish with as many yummy things as you can handle!

Peritas the Great

Alexander the Great—at his death ruler of a vast region spanning Macedonia to Persia—was one of history's most brilliant military minds and established the largest kingdom in the ancient world. He was the son of King Philip II, but some legends claim he was the child of the Greek god Zeus himself. His childhood teacher, Aristotle, tutored him in literature, science, and philosophy. Alexander also demonstrated a special connection with animals and tamed a wild stallion when he was just a teen. When Alexander became king at age 20, his beloved dog Peritas accompanied him in several wars. According to descriptions in these centuries-old stories, Peritas might have been either a Persian mastiff or a Molossus, an ancient Greek bulldog. In any case, he was enormously strong and supposedly killed a lion as well as protected Alexander from a war elephant by tearing at its lip as it charged him during a battle. The tales recount Peritas eventually being mortally wounded while fighting alongside the king and dying in his lap. The ruler was so overcome with grief that he founded a city in his dog's name, likely in what is modern-day Pakistan. This drink is complex yet laced with subtle flavors in honor of these warriors.

- 1½ ounces aquavit
- 1½ ounces rose water
- ¾ ounce honey cardamom syrup (add cardamom pods while heating syrup; see page 13 for syrup directions)
- ½ ounce freshly squeezed lemon juice
- Garnish: lemon wheel

Shake all ingredients with ice and strain into a cocktail glass. Garnish with the lemon wheel on the rim of the glass.

She-Wolf

Legend mixes with history in the story of Romulus and Remus, the brothers who founded Rome. Their grandfather, King Numitor, had been deposed by his younger brother Amulius. So when his daughter Rhea Silvia bore twin sons to the god Mars, Amulius damned her to the chaste life of a Vestal Virgin to prevent her from bearing more potential challengers to the throne. He also ordered the babies to be drowned in the Tiber River. However, as the fates would have it, the boys floated downstream until they encountered a female wolf, an animal sacred to Mars, who nursed them with her own milk until they were found and raised by a herdsman and his wife. When they grew up, they killed Amulius, which restored their grandfather as king. On the site where their wolf foster mother saved them, they erected a town with a great wall dividing it in two—one half for each brother to oversee. But, when Remus jumped over the wall, Romulus killed him and named the entire area Rome after himself. This drink is a slightly sweeter twist on the classic Italian Negroni in honor of the she-wolf who had more sweetness in her heart than the humans in this story.

- ¾ ounce gin
- ¾ ounce sweet vermouth
- ½ ounce Italian vanilla liqueur
- ½ ounce Italian artichoke liqueur
- Garnish: orange twist

Stir all ingredients with ice. Strain into a cocktail glass or over fresh ice in a double rocks glass. Place the twist on the edge of the glass or drop it in the drink.

Síoda's Soda

Irish President Michael Higgins is a renowned dog lover, and his pups often joined him for official business and press conferences. Also beloved by his constituents, they've served a purpose beyond simply being adorable, according to the president, who found comfort from his dogs when dealing with international affairs. He has been quoted as saying, "The dogs are not merely ice-breakers, they're also a great source of wisdom." When his Bernese mountain dog Síoda—meaning "silk" in Gaelic—passed away in 2020, the whole country took part in a national day of mourning. In early 2021, reporters heralded that Higgins had adopted a new Bernese mountain pup named Misneach, which translates to "courage." Clearly his dogs' names are chosen very thoughtfully because the puppy joined the president's other longtime companion Bród, meaning "pride." This drink is a play on a traditional Irish Coffee served as an iced soda and a liquid tribute to President Higgins's dearly departed dog.

- 3 ounces cold brew coffee
- 1½ ounces Irish whiskey
- 1 ounce brown sugar simple syrup (see page 13 for syrup directions)
- 1 ounce heavy cream
- 1½ ounces club soda
- Garnish: reusable metal straw (preferably green in honor of the Emerald Isle)

Shake all ingredients, except the soda, with ice. Pour half the club soda into a glass filled with fresh ice and then strain the mixture into the glass. Top with the rest of the club soda. Add the straw and give a light stir.

Rufuses-a-Plenty

Prime Minister Winston Churchill may have been nicknamed the British Bulldog, but it was his magnificent pet poodle Rufus who became known the world over during World War II. The dog joined him at luncheons and official meetings, was ever-present at family dinners, and sat on the prime minister's lap in the evenings. Churchill loved his dog so much that after Rufus was hit by a car in 1947, he also named his next poodle Rufus in the first dog's honor. But poodles were not the only sparkle in the great man's eye. Churchill famously loved Champagne, and some sources reckon he consumed over 42,000 bottles in his lifetime. He also particularly enjoyed Scotch, port, and brandy. This sparkling cocktail is worthy of a toast to the prime minister, who led Britain through World War II and was a devoted dog dad.

- 3 ounces Champagne, divided
- ½ ounce brandy
- ¾ ounce port
- Garnish: sugar rim

Moisten the rim of a Champagne flute or coupe with a slice of citrus or water, then dip it into granulated sugar. Start by gently pouring half of the Champagne into the glass. Add the brandy and port, then slowly top with the rest of the Champagne. This technique helps to control the bubbles and mixes the ingredients as they are added.

Nemo-la-la

French President Emmanuel Macron and First Lady Brigitte continued the tradition of having a first dog in the Élysée Palace. Their adorable black Labrador-griffon mix was adopted from the SPA Animal Refuge in Hermeray, just outside Paris. Since the 1970s, nearly all French presidents have had Labradors, but Nemo is likely the first one from a shelter. He was named after Captain Nemo from the Jules Verne novel *Twenty Thousand Leagues Under the Sea*, a favorite book of the president's. And Nemo has been considered a great ambassador in his post as first dog, appearing in videos about ending animal cruelty and abandonment in France. Like any true Frenchman, President Macron is also famously a wine lover and certainly aware that his country's fermented grape juice is the second-highest French export after aerospace technology. Saying "*Santé*" when clinking glasses in France means "to your health." So let's drink to the health of rescue dogs—and to the pleasure of sipping French wine throughout the world with this unique cocktail.

THE BETTER I GET TO KNOW MEN,
THE MORE I FIND MYSELF LOVING DOGS.

—CHARLES DE GAULLE,
PRESIDENT OF FRANCE'S FIFTH REPUBLIC

- 1 ounce Champagne
- 3 ounces French white wine (I love Vouvray for this drink.)
- ¾ ounce Calvados (French apple brandy)
- ¾ ounce peach liqueur
- Garnish: slice of peach

Pour the Champagne into a wine glass, then set aside. Shake the wine, Calvados, and peach liqueur with ice. Gently add to the mixture. Slide the peach slice onto the rim of the glass.

Candy Girl

Queen Elizabeth II, sovereign of the British Empire for seven decades, is often shown with her corgis. They are immortalized in paintings, photographs, and statues throughout her properties, and even the commemorative coin for the Queen's 50th Golden Jubilee depicts Her Royal Highness with a corgi. Her father, King George VI, brought the first corgi, named Dookie, to the House of Windsor in 1933 when the future monarch was only seven years old. After that, the queen owned more than 30 of them and, at times, there were upwards of five furbabies toddling around the palace. On her 18th birthday, she was given a Pembroke Welsh corgi named Susan, many of whose descendants have stayed within the royal family. In later years, the queen also took a liking to dorgis, a dachshund-corgi mix. The queen's drink of choice has been described as an aperitif of gin with Dubonnet, so this drink honors her preference in dogs—and drinks.

- 3 ounces Dubonnet (aromatic wine)
- 1 ounce London Dry gin
- Dash of orange bitters
- Garnish: lemon twist

Stir all ingredients with ice and strain into a cocktail glass. Place the lemon twist on the rim of the glass or drop it into the drink.

FROM PRUSSIA WITH LOVE

We all know that dogs are a (hu)man's best friend. But did you know that this sentiment was first voiced by King Frederick William II of Prussia in 1789 in reference to his beloved Italian greyhound? Apparently, his exact phrasing was: "The only absolute and best friend that a man has, in this selfish world, the only one that will not betray or deny him, is his *dog.*"

Bo's Honeypot

During his campaign for president, Barack Obama promised his daughters Malia and Sasha a dog once the race was over. So, in 2008, when the Obamas moved into the White House, he fulfilled that campaign promise and the family adopted Bo, a Portuguese water dog. The public was so interested in and enamored by Bo that the White House gift shop sold a stuffed animal in his likeness. In 2013, the Obamas adopted another dog named Sunny. Shortly thereafter, the Secret Service arrested kidnappers attempting to snatch the first dogs! As first lady, Michelle Obama's initiatives focused on improving American children's health and nutrition. To that end, she famously tended a vegetable garden on the White House grounds, which included thriving beehives. During the Obama tenure, a honey ale was made right on the property with honey from those hives. So for this drink I mixed mead, a beer-like drink brewed from honey, with the Portuguese fortified wine Madeira. Bo passed away in May 2021, so this drink is a tribute to that immensely popular former first dog.

IF YOU WANT A FRIEND IN WASHINGTON, GET A DOG.

—HARRY S. TRUMAN,
33RD PRESIDENT OF THE UNITED STATES

- 1 ounce Madeira
- ½ ounce fresh lemon juice
- 4 ounces mead
- Garnish: lemon wedge

Pour the Madeira into a pint glass. Add the lemon juice. Slowly add the mead until the glass is full. Place the lemon wedge on the rim of the glass.

Lion's Mane

Although canine fossils are found around the world, the shih tzu breed seems to have originated in Central Asia as evidenced by 3,000-year-old remains excavated in modern-day China. Buddhist tales speak of the Buddha riding a sacred lion, so these little dogs' lionlike manes have made them particularly favored by Chinese royalty for many centuries. Even the explorer Marco Polo spoke of small "lion dogs" kept in pens with captive hunting lions by Emperor Kublai Khan as far back as the 13th century. Their popularity skyrocketed, though, in the 1800s with the Empress Cixi, who was brought into Emperor Xianfeng's harem when she was 16 years old. Cixi came to power when Xianfeng died and her five-year-old son was next in line for the throne. A Buddhist leader of that time gave the empress dowager a pair of magnificent shih tzus, which created a lineage of palace dogs overseen by her chief eunuch. These furballs were often carried inside the robes of Chinese aristocracy in cold weather, because their thick fur generated heat. Although the empress was thought to be ruthless in order to maintain her power, she also made a royal decree punishing those unkind to animals, particularly the royal dogs. In honor of the fascinating history of the empress and her shih tzus, this drink is made with baijiu, a spirit widely consumed in China. Baijiu's malty, rich flavor—similar to genever or Scotch—is balanced with the citrusy yuzu in this recipe, also native to China.

- 2 ounces baijiu
- ¾ ounce yuzu puree (found online or in gourmet shops)
- Dash of orange bitters
- Garnish: lime wheel

Shake all ingredients with ice and strain into a cocktail glass. Garnish with the lime wheel on the rim of the glass.

"

I HAVE FOUND THAT WHEN YOU ARE DEEPLY TROUBLED,
THERE ARE THINGS YOU GET FROM THE SILENT DEVOTED
COMPANIONSHIP OF A DOG THAT YOU CAN GET
FROM NO OTHER SOURCE.

"

—DORIS DAY,
ACTRESS

FRIENDS IN HIGH PLACES

WE CHANGE A DOG'S LIFE FOR THE BETTER WHEN WE BRING
them home. Through volunteering and fostering, we can help even more animals
beyond the ones we've adopted. And each of us can advocate for the better treatment of animals in our communities. And then there are people who have the
power to positively impact many lives at once because they have a public platform.
To that end, it's heartening to see celebrities with large followings advocating for
dogs and other animals. With Hollywood being a dog-eat-dog environment, it's no
wonder that famous people value their faithful companions so much! Unlike the
fickle trappings of success, a dog doesn't care if their human is glamorous, rich, or

on the big screen. A dog doesn't care if someone has gained a few pounds, if their love life is a mess, or if their last project flopped. A homeless dog is just hoping to get the leading role in somebody's heart. These dog-loving celebrities know that even if the spotlight fades, the devotion from their faithful four-legged friend will not. Best of all, when stars advocate for animals, they can influence more people than most well-intentioned nonprofit campaigns could ever dream of reaching. They are truly using their positions for positive change in the world.

VIP (VERY IMPORTANT PET) TREATMENT

Your dog can feel like a star! With more people taking their canine companions with them on vacation, many high-end hotels now offer room service menus with special Puptails, such as bacon-infused water, and gourmet room service dog dishes, such as Doggie Tapas and Pupcakes, for your furry friend. Some even have plush doggie beds, doggie daycare, and walking services. Give your pet the escape of their dreams while you're free to do all the things you want to enjoy without worrying about your travel buddy back in the room.

Wine Down

We all secretly kinda wish we were besties with Drew Barrymore, don't we? Barrymore is cool, kind, active in social causes, and has a great sense of humor. The actress, movie producer, and talk show host has also been honored at the ASPCA Bergh Ball, which highlights individuals in entertainment and the arts who have made outstanding contributions to animal welfare. In her acceptance speech for the Compassion Award, she said: "There is such profoundness in connectivity and energy and altruism that we have with our animals, especially rescue animals, and they feel it back. And there is some level of symbiotic gratitude because you do save each other." It's safe to say that any dog owner can relate to this sentiment. Although Barrymore does not always drink alcohol, she has been a partner in a female-owned wine company, so I created this wine-based cocktail to toast this animal advocate celebrity gal pal.

DOGS NEVER BITE ME. JUST HUMANS.

—MARILYN MONROE, ACTRESS

- 6 raspberries
- 6 mint leaves
- 4 ounces rosé wine
  (or sub nonalcoholic wine)
- Garnish: Pinch of grated lemon zest

Muddle raspberries and mint leaves in the bottom of a cocktail shaker. Add the wine, then shake well with ice. Strain into an ice-filled white wine glass. Sprinkle lemon zest on the surface of the drink.

Golden Gal

No matter how many birthdays Betty White celebrated, she will eternally remain America's Sweetheart. In 1930, White began her career at eight years old on the radio. Since then, her television career spanned 80 years—more than any other actor in that medium. From boomers to Gen Z, White's personality delighted all audiences and defies age. Most of us know her best from *The Golden Girls*, but did you know that back in the 1970s she also produced and hosted a TV show called *The Pet Set*, where celebrities showed off their furry friends? Her interest in animal welfare—both domesticated and wild—developed during family vacations in the mountains around Southern California when she dreamed of a career as a park ranger. White served on the board of the Los Angeles Zoo since 1974 and was involved with American Humane, which is responsible for the trademarked certification "no animals were harmed" at the end of films and TV shows in which animals appear. And, White was never a wallflower—the good-timing gal often remarked that she enjoyed vodka with lots of lemon and that her favorite drink was a Vodka Martini. This recipe is created in your memory, Betty!

- 1½ ounces citron vodka
- ¾ ounce limoncello
- ½ ounce freshly squeezed lemon juice
- Garnish: lemon wedge

Shake all ingredients with ice and strain into a cocktail glass. Place the lemon wedge on the rim of the glass.

WILL IT

You don't have to be a celebrity to protect your furry family after you're gone. Many animals land in shelters when their human passes away without a plan in place. A will must include two essential elements: 1. A designated caregiver who agrees ahead of time to take your pet in if you become incapacitated or pass on. 2. A sum of money set aside to help that caregiver pay for food and vet bills. Also consider leaving a legacy gift to your favorite animal rescue or shelter.

Dirty Little Secrets

If you were a devotee of this straight-shooting comedienne's late-night show in the mid-2000s, you'll remember Chelsea Handler's rescue dog Chunk. The lovable German shepherd–chow mix often trotted across the stage with as much charisma as the celebrity guests. He also appeared on the cover of Handler's saucy autobiographical essay book *Chelsea Chelsea Bang Bang*. When he and Tammy, Chelsea's other rescue dog at that time, passed away, Handler vowed to adopt more dogs from shelters as soon as possible. Enter Bert and Bernice, brother and sister chow chows, who are a prominent part of Handler's spill-all memoir *Life Will Be the Death of Me*. This dog-loving, smack-talking firecracker feminist inspires the rest of us to live out loud, unapologetically. Her second book *Are You There, Vodka? It's Me, Chelsea* is the inspiration for this drink, because it is spicy, strong, a little bit dirty, and just might lead to a few oh-so-good bad decisions!

IF THERE ARE NO DOGS IN HEAVEN, THEN WHEN I DIE, I WANT TO GO WHERE THEY WENT.

—WILL ROGERS, ACTOR

- 3 ounces vodka
- ½ ounce olive brine
- Dash of hot sauce
- Garnish: olives on a toothpick or cocktail skewer

Shake all ingredients with ice and strain into a cocktail glass. Serve with an olive garnish on the rim of the glass.

Super Soul Spaniel

Despite being one of the wealthiest people on the planet, Oprah Winfrey has always paid respect to the people and places in her rearview mirror. Winfrey remains active with causes in her hometown. In 2008, she heard about PAWS Chicago, a no-kill shelter—which means that they do not put animals to sleep in order to make space for more admissions. However, this noble practice also means that they face the financial challenges of housing and feeding animals for longer periods. Winfrey's own gorgeous spaniels often appear in her magazine, where she has been quoted as saying, "Nothing makes me happier than being with my dogs." After Winfrey enlisted journalist Lisa Ling to expose the cruel conditions dogs endure in puppy mills and the millions of perfectly healthy dogs euthanized each year because they have nowhere to go, she decided to feature PAWS Chicago on her show to help their great work get more exposure. Winfrey even sponsored a room at that shelter in honor of her late beloved dog Sophie and adopted her next dogs—Sadie, Sunny, and Lauren—from PAWS Chicago as well. Ms. O is also known to enjoy tequila and indulge in a little downtime in her own beautiful gardens where inspiration often comes to her. In this drink, I incorporated wildflowers to help inspire one of those "aha moments" she has spoken about so often on her Super Soul podcast.

- 2 ounces chamomile tea
- 1½ ounces tequila
- 1½ ounces pineapple juice
- 1 ounce pomegranate juice
- ¾ ounce elderflower liqueur
- Garnish: edible flowers

Shake all ingredients with ice and strain into a cocktail glass or in a tall glass filled with fresh ice. Garnish with edible flowers on the surface of the drink or frozen into ice cubes.

Purple Pup Star

For Gen X, Prince was one of a handful of megastars who defined a generation. Most of us who grew up in the '80s had at least one high school makeout sesh to his album *Purple Rain*, and at the time, people often joked that he was one of few men who could wear makeup and heels and still steal any guy's girlfriend. He also wrote a very edgy song against animal abuse called "Animal Kingdom," which was played at the PETA (People for the Ethical Treatment of Animals) 20th anniversary party in New York in 2000. Prince is quoted as saying that "compassion is an action word without boundaries," which can be understood as trying to implement all the changes possible for the betterment of animal welfare. He even called for an annual Animal Rights Day that would close all slaughterhouses for 24 hours on a designated day every year to highlight the killing of the millions of animals humans eat, something that most people take for granted. PETA went on to name him the "Sexiest Vegetarian Celebrity" in 2006. Prince didn't drink much alcohol, so this tribute drink is a mocktail made with purple grape juice as a nod to his iconic pop album mentioned above.

- 3 ounces purple grape juice
- 1½ ounces cherry juice
- ½ ounce fresh lime juice
- Garnish: make grape ice cubes by placing one grape into each opening of an ice tray, then cover with water and freeze

Shake all juices with ice, then strain into a wine goblet. Add the grape ice cubes.

DOGS HAVE A WAY OF FINDING THE PEOPLE
WHO NEED THEM AND FILLING AN EMPTINESS
WE DIDN'T EVER KNOW WE HAD.

—THOM JONES, WRITER

CHAPTER
8

RAISE THE *WOOF!* EVERY HOLIDAY IS A *PAWLIDAY*

EVERY DAY WE GET TO SPEND WITH OUR DOG IS A SPECIAL occasion. Dogs live in the moment—a great reminder for their human guardians. Still, for those designated days of the year when humans gather to eat, drink, and be merry, a cocktail is a welcome addition to the festivities. Each year's celebrations, big and small, are a great time to reflect, rejoice, and renew ourselves with those we love, including our doggos! These dog-themed holiday drinks feature some larger batch recipes so you are ready for a party, but any drink in this book can be scaled up by replacing ounce measurements with cups if you're mixing for a group. Sip your way through the year with a smile, a shake, and a stir . . . and, hopefully, if you're lucky, a few wagging tails and sloppy kisses.

Lucky Dog

Most of us start a new year with grand plans and hopes for a bit of good luck along the way. Starting new challenges, setting career goals, or just promising ourselves to take more time off to chill with our furry friends—it feels good to be awash in overwhelming optimism. To paraphrase the popular saying, "Good luck is the sum of preparedness meeting opportunity, but a happy wink from the universe never hurts." In the Chinese calendar, the next Year of the Dog rolls around in 2030, and like our canine buddies, those born that year will be brave, loyal, clever, and lively. Many countries in Asia celebrate the Chinese New Year or their own version of it, and the Korean New Year usually aligns with the Chinese one. Soju is a Korean distillate made from rice and grains, and its popularity has spread from Asia to mixology bars across the rest of the world in recent years. This lucky dog cocktail—made with yogurt and fresh fruit—is a common style of drink in South Korea and sure to get your tail wagging with good fortune for the upcoming year.

- 3 ounces soju
- 3 tablespoons yogurt (plain or flavored with honey or fruit)
- ½ ounce freshly squeezed lemon juice
- Garnish: 1 whole strawberry

Vigorously shake the soju, yogurt, and lemon juice with ice, then strain into a cocktail glass. Make one slice in the strawberry—halfway up to its stem—and slide it onto the rim of the glass.

Doggie Style

Whether you're madly in love, head-over-heels in lust, or write Valentine's Day off as a consumer holiday for chocolatiers and greeting card companies, we can all agree that the saying "*Netflix and chill*" takes on a whole new meaning when rewatching your favorite rom-coms with your one true love—that's right, your dog. No matter what your plans, Valentine's Day is a great excuse to chow down on chocolate and indulge in all the things that make you feel loved, most especially that furry face who will always consider you the love of their life. This drink has dreamy chocolate, rich cream, and a swirl of raspberry liqueur to toast all the yumminess your heart could desire.

- 1½ ounces vodka
- 1½ ounces chocolate liqueur
- ½ ounce heavy cream
- ¾ ounce raspberry liqueur
- Garnish: cherry (fresh, Maraschino, or chocolate-covered)

Shake all ingredients with ice and strain into a cocktail glass. Drop the cherry into the drink.

Wolfhounds and Serpents

Although, in the United States, St. Patrick's Day is an excuse to guzzle green beer, the early life of the saint is far more interesting. Captured in his native Scotland and sold into slavery in Ireland, he worked as a shepherd, where his only companions were large Irish wolfhounds to whom he would practice giving religious sermons in Celtic. One night, he had a prophetic dream in which his favorite dog appeared as an angel instructing him to escape to the coast to find freedom. The next morning, he took this advice seriously and fled. According to legend, at the shore he found a band of pirates who had captured 100 wild dogs but couldn't sail away because the terrified dogs—who had been wrangled onto the boat—barked and growled and wouldn't let them aboard. Because Patrick had a miraculous way with dogs after years of solitary life with them, he offered to calm them in exchange for safe passage to the continent where he could find his freedom. Centuries later, he was proclaimed a saint in Ireland as he had managed to unite pagan beliefs with those of Christianity. And, in another act of divinity, he is said to have banished all the serpents (representing the Devil) from Ireland. This drink is made with Irish poitín—a countryside moonshine mostly made from barley, as is Scotch—making it particularly applicable for St. Patrick.

- 1½ ounces poitín
- 1 ounce Irish breakfast tea, sweetened to taste
- ¾ ounce green melon liqueur
- ½ ounce freshly squeezed lemon juice
- Garnish: honeydew melon balls

Shake all ingredients with ice and strain into a cocktail glass. Garnish with melon balls on a skewer or dropped into the drink.

Yankee Doodle Dog

In recent years, "doodle" dogs of all kinds have exploded in popularity due to their friendly temperament, cute looks, and minimal shedding. Doodles love to play and socialize and are a great addition to a summer backyard barbecue, which are particularly popular in the United States around the July Fourth Independence Day celebrations. This fun drink is a riff from the song "Yankee Doodle Dandy," and the Pop Rocks crackle on your tongue just as sparklers crackle in the sky. (Note: Always keep dogs inside during fireworks as most are frightened by the loud noises and could get hurt or injured.)

**ONCE YOU'VE HAD A WONDERFUL DOG,
A LIFE WITHOUT ONE IS A LIFE DIMINISHED.**

....

—DEAN KOONTZ, MYSTERY NOVELIST

- 1½ ounces cherry vodka
- ¾ ounce blue curaçao
- ½ ounce freshly squeezed lime juice
- Garnish: whipped cream and Pop Rocks

Moisten the rim of a cocktail glass with a piece of citrus fruit or water, then dip it into Pop Rocks. Set aside. Shake all ingredients with ice, then gently strain into the rimmed glass and add a dollop of whipped cream on the surface of the drink.

Bitches Brew

For centuries, witches have been feared by common folk because they are believed to have supernatural powers through which they can communicate with animals and manipulate humans. Some think witches can see the future or communicate without words via telepathic abilities. Many of us with dogs could swear they are telepathic too! Have you noticed that your dog decides if a person is likable or not within seconds of meeting them? There are many stories of dogs having a spooky sixth sense and psychically knowing things that seem unperceivable. For example, Rudolph Valentino—a famous Italian sex symbol from the 1920s silent film era—was so close with his Alsatian Doberman named Kabar that the dog reportedly let out a bloodcurdling howl at the exact moment the actor died in New York—and Kabar was in Los Angeles. Creepy! The animal kingdom clearly has extraordinary skills we humans lack, so to honor their witchy wonders, fill your Halloween cauldron with this ghoulishly delicious punch made with pisco, a South American brandy.

- 4 cups pineapple juice
- 3 cups pisco
- 2 cups watermelon juice
- ¾ cup freshly squeezed lemon juice
- Garnish: Make a "bloody" hand by freezing cherry juice in a plastic glove, then cutting the glove off to drop the hand ice mold into the punch. As the hand melts, it will continue to flavor the punch with juice.

Pour all ingredients into a punch bowl and add the cherry ice hand at the last minute as guests arrive.

Lil' Punkin

Thanksgiving is the American holiday known for stuffing ourselves with turkey, corn, and desserts galore; but somewhere in our collective gluttony there is the beautiful tradition of setting aside this day every year to express gratitude for all we have. We give thanks for our blessings such as health, a home, and our loved ones—including our dogs. When cooking up the pumpkin pie, set aside some pumpkin flesh (raw or cooked) for your canine friends. It can be mixed into their food (maybe some turkey, too!) or baked into doggie treats. This pumpkin cocktail makes a delicious liquid dessert or a festive indulgence while watching the big annual football game. It is also quite delicious as a mocktail for nondrinkers if you follow these directions and substitute apple cider for vodka.

- 1½ ounces caramel-flavored vodka
- 1 ounce sweetened condensed milk (or coconut cream)
- 1 ounce pureed (or canned) pumpkin
- ¾ ounce maple syrup
- ½ ounce fresh lemon juice
- Dash each of cinnamon, nutmeg, and clove
- Garnish: vanilla cookie crumb rim

Moisten the rim of a cocktail glass with a piece of citrus or water and dip into the crushed vanilla cookie crumbs, then set aside. Shake all ingredients including the baking spices vigorously with ice. Gently strain into the rimmed glass.

Max's Matcha Nog

Bustling holiday entertaining can bring out the Grinch in anyone, but a few sips of this creamy and delicious matcha green tea eggnog will please even the crankiest curmudgeon. Dr. Seuss's classic holiday tale *How the Grinch Stole Christmas* stirs the hearts of dog lovers when they meet Max, the Grinch's hapless sidekick. Even when the Grinch is devising evil plans, his dog faithfully stands by him, seeing only the best in his less-than-ideal buddy. Max's dreams are finally realized when the Grinch turns himself around and his heart swells in that furry green chest. This drink is green like the Grinch but sweet like Max, and serves two to three people. For a bigger batch, simply translate ounces to cups and count one egg per person for the larger quantity.

- 2 large eggs, separated
- ⅛ cup granulated sugar
- 1 teaspoon ground nutmeg
- 2 tablespoons matcha powder (found at supermarkets)
- 8 ounces coconut milk
- 2 ounces heavy cream (or coconut creamer)
- 2 ounces white rum
- 2 ounces pisco
- Garnish: candy canes

First separate your eggs with the egg whites in one bowl and the yolks in another. Beat the egg whites with a mixer on high speed until they start to get stiff (about 3 to 5 minutes), then set aside. Beat the egg yolks with the sugar for one minute, then add the nutmeg, matcha powder, coconut milk, heavy cream, and liquors. Slowly fold in the egg whites. For individual servings, ladle 4 ounces of the mixture into a cocktail shaker, then shake with ice and strain into a cocktail glass. For a large batch, refrigerate the mixture until ready to serve. Stir well to recombine and ladle into individual cups. Place a cane on the rim of each cocktail glass or punch cup when serving.

Santa Paws

Whether you celebrate Christmas, Hanukkah, Kwanzaa, or the Winter Solstice, or simply love exchanging presents and snuggling your favorite dog under the mistletoe, this cozy cocktail is perfect for sipping in snowy weather. Mulled wine is traditional at winter holiday parties and fills the house with the homey aroma of baking spices. And, of course, in the parts of the world where December is the middle of summer, this can also be a delicious sangria-style drink over ice.

THE GIFT WHICH I AM SENDING YOU IS CALLED A DOG AND IS, IN FACT, THE MOST PRECIOUS AND VALUABLE POSSESSION OF MANKIND.

—THEODORUS GAZA, 15TH CENTURY GREEK SCHOLAR

- 1 bottle (750 ml) inexpensive red wine (save the expensive wine to drink with dinner!)
- 1 cup brandy
- 1 cup brewed black tea (or brewed chai tea for more flavorful spices)
- 1 cup orange juice
- 6 ounces honey syrup (see page 13 for syrup directions)
- 8 whole cloves
- 8 star anise
- 4 cinnamon sticks
- Garnish: orange wheels or cinnamon sticks

Pour all ingredients into a pot on the stove over low heat or in a slow cooker to keep the mixture warm, stirring occasionally. Ladle into bar mugs or coffee cups. Place an orange wheel and/or a cinnamon stick into each cup when serving. If preparing as a sangria, mix all ingredients in a large pitcher and pour into ice-filled wine glasses.

"

DOGS' LIVES ARE SHORT, TOO SHORT,
BUT YOU KNOW THAT GOING IN. YOU KNOW THE PAIN IS
COMING, YOU'RE GOING TO LOSE A DOG, AND THERE'S
GOING TO BE GREAT ANGUISH, SO YOU LIVE FULLY IN
THE MOMENT WITH HER, NEVER FAIL TO SHARE HER JOY
OR DELIGHT IN HER INNOCENCE, BECAUSE YOU CAN'T
SUPPORT THE ILLUSION THAT A DOG CAN BE YOUR LIFELONG
COMPANION. THERE'S SUCH BEAUTY IN THE HARD HONESTY
OF THAT, IN ACCEPTING AND GIVING LOVE WHILE ALWAYS
AWARE THAT IT COMES WITH AN UNBEARABLE PRICE.
MAYBE LOVING DOGS IS A WAY WE DO PENANCE FOR ALL THE
OTHER ILLUSIONS WE ALLOW OURSELVES AND THE MISTAKES
WE MAKE BECAUSE OF THOSE ILLUSIONS.

"

—DEAN KOONTZ,
BEST-SELLING AUTHOR

DRINKING TO YOUR DOG: CREATE A SIGNATURE COCKTAIL

AUGUST 26 IS INTERNATIONAL DOG DAY, AND PEOPLE AROUND the world post photos of their pups on social media and raise a glass to your furry friend and raise money for dogs in need. Would you like to take it a step further? I've created countless signature cocktails for celebrity-studded events, animal shelter fundraisers, birthday parties, weddings, and corporate events. I've even taught home bartenders how to create their own drinks in The Liquid Muse cocktail classes, both live and online. Immortalizing your pup with a signature cocktail is a fun way to show how much you love them. So, in this section I'll help you design a drink to pair with a tribute to your dog for International Dog Day, your dog's birthday, their adoption anniversary, or any other doggone reason. To commemorate your dog's "Gotcha Day," you could even host a cocktail party featuring your special drink and ask guests to bring donations for your local shelter in your pooch's honor.

If you have never bartended or created a recipe before, don't worry. Personalizing a cocktail is simple when you start with a classic recipe and then swap out like-for-like ingredients. Think of cocktail making like cooking. For example, a chocolate chip cookie dough recipe will always have the same ratios of flour to salt to butter to eggs. That foundation doesn't change. However, the personalization happens when you swap butterscotch chips for chocolate or add pecans or make those kinds of small adjustments. You can do the same with a cocktail recipe by switching out the base spirit, in the same proportion, for another one—e.g., replacing vodka with whiskey—or changing out the liqueur, but in the same amount. Below are some instructions and inspirations to point you in the right direction.

1. Pick your spirit. Do you love rum? Are you a whiskey aficionado? Is tequila your go-to? Start with the spirit you want to use as a base for your drink and work from there.

2. What are some of your favorite classic cocktails? Do you love Mai Tais? Manhattans? Cosmopolitans? Look up the original recipe and see the ratios of spirit to other ingredients. Then experiment by replacing vodka with pisco or raspberry liqueur with chocolate liqueur.

3. What kind of glass will you use and how will it be served? Will it be straight up in a cocktail coupe? Or poured over ice in a tall Collins glass?

4. What kind of garnish will you choose to make your drink more impressive? A piece of fruit? A flower? Fancy ice? A sugar or candy rim?

5. When coming up with a name, consider the following for inspiration: What is the name of your dog? How would you describe your dog's personality? What style of drink are you making? (Tropical? Sophisticated? Classic? Inspired by a film or character?)

Let these directions get you shaking and impressing your pals in no time. Or, toast your pooch while hanging at home hosting a cocktail party for just the two of you. Either way, we dog lovers know that anything is more fun when our furry companions are with us. From our (dog) house to yours, Lula and I raise a glass to you both—and wish you many adventures over the years to come.

Acknowledgments

I thank my mom, Sylvia, who raised my sister and me to love animals and showed us, by example, that there is always room for "one more." I also toast my dad, Pierre, who shares my fondness for Manhattans, which we enjoy making when we get together. One day, I look forward to sharing animal activism (and eventually, a cocktail) with my niece, Ava.

This book would not have come to life without our talented (all-female) publishing team: my agent, Lilly Ghahremani; editor, Jordana Hawkins; designer, Frances Soo Ping Chow; production editor, Amber Morris; and illustrator, Rae Ritchie.

Index

About
the Author

Natalie Bovis is an award-winning mixologist, event producer, and author. She was one of the first women to blog about mixology when she launched The Liquid Muse in 2006. Since then, she has written for dozens of magazines, cofounded OM Chocolate Liqueur, and created the annual Cocktails & Culture Festival featuring chefs, mixologists, artists, and its popular TACO WARS competition. Natalie produces culinary and creativity retreats for the public, and fundraising dinners for nonprofits, including the James Beard Foundation. She teaches live and online cocktail and cooking classes, consults for global food and beverage brands, and shakes drinks on television shows across the United States. Natalie is first-generation American with an English mum and French dad and has lived and worked in Santa Fe, Los Angeles, Paris, Washington, DC, and the Costa Brava (Spain). She has seven rescue pets (not counting the thirteen fish), fosters kittens, and often donates proceeds from her events to animal welfare organizations. Natalie's other passions include traveling, cooking, hiking, and writing poetry and romance novels as well as food, travel, and self-improvement guides. Her previous cocktail books include *Preggatinis: Mixology for the Mom-to-Be, The Bubbly Bride: Your Ultimate Wedding Cocktail Guide,* and *Edible Cocktails: From Garden to Glass.* Share more cocktail fun with Natalie at TheLiquidMuse.com.

NATALIE BOVIS is a beverage/food/ travel writer, culinary event producer, and cofounder of OM Chocolate Liqueur. She is the bestselling author of *Preggatinis*, *The Bubbly Bride*, and *Edible Cocktails*. Learn more at TheLiquidMuse.com.